A Confederate in Paris

A Confederate in Paris:

Letters of A. Dudley Mann 1867-1879

Edited by

Karen Stokes

A Confederate in Paris: Letters of A. Dudley Mann 1867-1879

Copyright© 2024 by *Karen Stokes*

ALL RIGHTS RESERVED. No part of this publication may be reproduced, distributed, or transmitted in any form or by any means, including photocopying, recording, or other electronic or mechanical methods, or by any information storage and retrieval system without the prior written permission of the publisher, except in the case of very brief quotations embodied in critical reviews and certain other non-commercial uses permitted by copyright law.

Produced in the Republic of South Carolina by

SHOTWELL PUBLISHING LLC

Post Office Box 2592

Columbia, So. Carolina 29202

www.ShotwellPublishing.com

On the Cover: Carte de visite photograph of A. Dudley Mann taken by the Le Jeune studio in Paris, in or after 1872. It was owned by Mrs. Varina Davis. Courtesy of the Virginia Museum of History and Culture. Panorama pris du Châtelet courtesy of Wikimedia.

ISBN: 978-1-947660-97-7

FIRST EDITION

10 9 8 7 6 5 4 3 2

Contents

Acknowledgments vi

Editorial Method................................. vii

Introduction 1

Ambrose Dudley Mann's Letters
to Mrs. Keitt, 1867-1879 31

Epilogue 141

Appendix 143

Bibliography 155

About the Editor 161

Acknowledgments

THIS BOOK WOULD NOT HAVE BEEN POSSIBLE without Catherine G. Rogers, who preserved the papers of Sue Sparks Keitt for many years and donated them to the South Carolina Historical Society in 2020. The editor is also indebted to her for providing the initial transcriptions of Mann's letters, which were a great help as the final transcription and editing was done. Thanks are also due to Hubert Leroy of the Confederate Historical Association of Belgium (CHAB), Lucienne Jean of the Association Lamorlaye Memoire & Accueil (ALMA), Patricia Kruger, and Brooke Guthrie of the David M. Rubenstein Rare Book and Manuscript Library at Duke University. I will always remember the interest and kindness of Daniel Frankingnoul of CHAB, who passed away in 2023. He studied Ambrose Dudley Mann for many years and graciously lent his expertise by reading a draft of the introduction and offering helpful suggestions and information.

Editorial Method

THE LETTERS WERE TRANSCRIBED as written except for datelines, which have been standardized, and the omission of dashes as punctuation. The small, often minute handwriting of Ambrose Dudley Mann can be very difficult to decipher, and non-italicized words or phrases in brackets represent the editor's best interpretation. Most of the letters were accompanied by envelopes, information from which was used in the headings of each letter in the text.

Introduction

IN FEBRUARY 1861, when Jefferson Davis was elected as the president of the Confederate States of America, one of his first official acts was to commission several men as envoys to European governments for the purpose of seeking recognition for the new republic. One of these commissioners was Ambrose Dudley Mann, who had formerly served as a United States diplomat and as the first Assistant Secretary of State under President Franklin Pierce. Mann left on his mission to Europe in March 1861, and would never again set foot on American soil.

Jefferson Davis had met Mann while serving as the Secretary of War in the Pierce cabinet, and the two men quickly became close friends. Among Mann's other friends in Washington was Laurence Massillon Keitt, who began his service in the U.S. House of Representatives for South Carolina's third congressional district in 1853. In 1859, Keitt brought his beautiful bride Susan Sparks Keitt to the national capital, where she soon became a popular society belle. James Buchanan, who had assumed the presidency of the United States in March 1857, greatly admired her. Susan's husband wrote to his family that the old bachelor president had "taken a chivalric devotion to her," and that Buchanan told everyone that she was "the most cultivated and fascinating woman" he had ever met in Washington.[1] Mrs. Keitt also made a conquest in Ambrose Dudley Mann, who became her fervently devoted admirer, friend, and correspondent. Their friendship remained strong after the war, and although separated by thousands of miles, they continued to write to each other, as documented in this collection of Mann's letters to Mrs. Keitt—which also reveal that what he called his "almost idolatrous love" for her never diminished.

---

[1] Merchant, *South Carolina Fire-Eater*, 124-125.

Ambrose Dudley Mann

Ambrose Dudley Mann's character presented some interesting if somewhat dissonant qualities. He was cosmopolitan, yet a devout Christian; and, as a high-toned, chivalrous Southern gentleman, he was something of an aristocrat, yet a passionate adherent of Jeffersonian republicanism, which emphasized limited, decentralized government and popular sovereignty (that is, government by consent of the governed). His detractors criticized him for a number of faults including grandiloquence in his speech and writing, but Varina Davis, the wife of his close friend Jefferson Davis, described him as "a perfect man" who had "every Christian virtue."[2] Mann's Christian faith is evident in his letters, but they also offer ample evidence of his two principal earthly passions—Mrs. Keitt, and the Southern (Jeffersonian) ideal of government.

Mann was born in or near Hanover Courthouse, Virginia, on April 26, 1801.[3] His Virginia ancestry has been described as aristocratic, and he wrote to Mrs. Keitt in 1869 that he was "descended paternally from a family of the 'Kentish men'" of England, but little is actually known about his forebears.[4] A brief biographical sketch about him appears in the *Mann Memorial,* a genealogy of the Mann family published in 1884, but the book does not connect him with any other member of the family, and the identity of his parents still remains a mystery. Biographical details about his youth are sketchy, but his family apparently moved from Virginia to Kentucky when he was a boy, and in his early teenage years, he was an apprentice to the publisher of the *Guardian of Liberty,* the first newspaper in Cynthiana, Kentucky. His fellow apprentice, Hubbard H. Kavanaugh,

---

2   Davis, *Jefferson Davis,* 1: 556-67.
3   The date of 1801 is generally accepted as the birth year of Ambrose Dudley Mann, although a few sources give his birth year as 1805, such as an article in *The Illustrated London News* (May 4, 1861). In a letter to Mrs. Keitt (27 August 1868), Mann mentioned that he was seven years old at the time of the War of 1812.
4   "An English scholar has argued that the social, political, and ideological pattern of the Old South was firmly impressed on seventeenth-century Virginia by the early colonists, a great many of whom came from the county of Kent ... It gave birth to various forms of Southern political philosophy, all of which in one way or another emphasized states' rights or state sovereignty." Johnson, *North Against South,* 73-74.

later recalled: "Though we were but boys, then but recently in our teens, he was so peculiar that he made a lasting impression upon my mind. He was singularly ambitious and aspiring. He seemed resolved to be great. As a printer, he looked to Ben Franklin as his model man. I thought he had capacity, if persistent in the means, at least, to reach distinction."[5]

Mann received an appointment to the U.S. Military Academy at West Point in 1823 but soon resigned, leaving in 1824. According to a biography of Jefferson Davis, Mann had previously attended Transylvania University in Lexington, Kentucky, where he would have been required to master the Greek and Latin classics, higher mathematics, and ancient and modern geography and history.[6] In 1830 Mann was still living in Kentucky, where he married Hebe L. Carter, the daughter of Robert Wormley Carter of Virginia, and the granddaughter of William Grayson, a Revolutionary War officer and Virginia senator.[7] Their son William Grayson Mann was born in 1833.

Mann apparently practiced law in Kentucky for a while, and also entered into unsuccessful business ventures in Owingsville and Greenup County. He was active in politics, however, and his services to the Democratic Party probably led President John Tyler to appoint him as consul to Bremen in 1842. This was the first of a series of diplomatic posts and assignments for Mann, including a notable mission to the German Confederation to negotiate commercial treaties. His wife Hebe passed away in 1849, and both before and after her death his son "Willie" accompanied him on many of his diplomatic travels. Educated by European tutors, Willie acted as his father's interpreter and secretary from his early teenage years. He became an attorney, and in 1860 he was practicing law in New Orleans, Louisiana, as the partner of Robert Nash Ogden, Jr.[8]

---

5   Perrin, *History of Bourbon, Scott, Harrison and Nicholas Counties,* 274.
6   Allen, *Unconquerable Heart,* 221.
7   Ambrose Dudley Mann was sometimes referred to as Colonel Mann, a designation arising from his service as an officer in the Kentucky militia.
8   Daniel Frankignoul found William Grayson Mann listed as the law partner of Robert N. Ogden in an 1860 New Orleans city directory. Frankignoul, Daniel. "A. Dudley Mann." Message to the editor, 7 March 2021. E-mail.

In 1853, President Franklin Pierce appointed Mann to the newly created office of Assistant Secretary of State. After Mann resigned this post in 1855, his main pursuit became the establishment of a steamship company that would operate between Chesapeake Bay and the United Kingdom. He wrote articles advocating for this direct line of trade between the Southern states and Europe in order to reduce the South's dependence on Northern shipping and promote the region's economic independence. Northern firms, especially those in New York City, dominated shipping and trade in the United States, taking in enormous profits, and Southerners saw themselves becoming impoverished while the North was being enriched at their expense. Historian Sven Beckert noted that many New York cotton traders "earned remarkable profits because their capital was so desperately needed in the South and because they had a hand in each step of the trade, most notably a virtual stranglehold on the regularly scheduled ships shuttling between northern, southern, and European ports."[9]

In 1856, inspired by the colossal iron steam ship the *Great Eastern* that he had seen under construction in England, Mann published an open letter in *DeBow's Review* in which "he advocated the use of four ships of her size on a weekly service from Chesapeake Bay to Milford Haven [Wales]."[10] In another article published in *DeBow's Review* in 1858, Mann stated that the purpose of this direct trade enterprise was to deliver the South from "commercial inequality in this Union."[11] Mann was instrumental in the establishment of the Atlantic Steam Ferry Company in Virginia in 1858, but because of the advent of the war and other problems, the company was short-lived.[12]

Mann's loyalty and devotion to the South did not waver when seven Southern states seceded and formed their own confederacy in 1861. In a reminiscence published in 1896, William Grayson Mann

---

9   Beckert, *The Monied Metropolis,* 22.
10 Tyler, *Steam Conquers the Atlantic,* 294.
11 Mann, "Southern Direct Trade with Europe," 353.
12 A recent historical novel by Paul Stack, *The Leviathan,* features Ambrose Dudley Mann as one its main characters. Stack makes the case that Mann was involved in a secret plan to bring the *Great Eastern* to a Southern port in 1861.

recalled the sequence of events that led to a reprise of his father's diplomatic career, this time as an envoy of the Confederate States of America.[13] In February 1861, William Grayson Mann was living in New Orleans, and he accompanied the Louisiana delegation to the Confederate provisional congress in Montgomery, Alabama, where he had a conversation with the newly inaugurated president, Jefferson Davis. Davis asked him to send a telegraph to his father in Washington informing him that he had been appointed as "the first commissioner of the confederacy to represent it abroad." Mann's reminiscence continued:

> I followed out his instructions and at the very hour when the message was received at my father's hotel he was at the white house, whither he had been summoned by President Buchanan. The cabinet was then in session and my father was invited into the conference and informed that, although it was well known that his sympathies were with the south, the confidence of the chief executive and his official advisers in my father's integrity and loyalty was such as to influence them to request him to undertake a most important mission to England. Then he was told that in the brief time before Mr. Buchanan must give place to Abraham Lincoln, it had been determined to secure, if possible, the good offices of Queen Victoria as a mediator between the north and south, hoping thereby to avoid bloodshed.[14] He was informed that his letters of credit were ready; that brief instructions had already been drawn up by the Secretary of State and that he must come to an immediate decision in order to embark upon his journey that night.

---

13 William Grayson Mann's reminiscence, "The Life of a Diplomat," which was published in a Savannah newspaper, is reproduced in full in the appendix to this book.

14 President Buchanan had formerly served as the U.S. minister to the Court of St. James for three years and was well acquainted with Queen Victoria. In 1858, Buchanan and the British queen exchanged the first transatlantic telegram, but the cable failed soon afterward, and the transatlantic telegraphic service did not resume until 1866.

His reply was he must have a few moments for reflection—and with that answer of indecision he returned to his hotel. There he found awaiting him my message, sent at the request of Mr. Davis. His sympathies with the south were too strong to be resisted and he immediately signified his acceptance of the mission offered by the confederacy and notified President Buchanan of an unfavorable decision regarding the latter's request.

Two other commissioners, the brilliant and eloquent William L. Yancey and Judge Alfred B. Rost, were also named by Mr. Davis as commissioners of the confederacy to the European powers and at his personal appointment I was made secretary to my father.[15]

Mann and the other two Confederate commissioners arrived in London in April 1861, and the following month, on May 4, they met informally with Lord Russell, the British Foreign Secretary, on the question of recognition for the Confederacy. Later that year, knowing that Europe was kept informed of events in America almost exclusively by Northern newspapers, Mann managed to work out an arrangement with the Reuters news agency in London to receive reports from Southern sources. In September 1861, the Confederate Secretary of State ordered Mann to go to Belgium, where he attempted to secure recognition for the Confederacy from King Leopold I.

In the winter of 1863-1864, he was sent to Rome as a special envoy to Pope Pius IX. At the Vatican, Mann once again sought recognition for his government. He also endeavored to persuade the Pope to use his influence to prevent the enlistment of Irish and German Catholics in the army of the United States. In a letter to Confederate Secretary of State Judah P. Benjamin dated November 14, 1863, he reported the details of his audience with the Pope. With his son as interpreter, Mann explained to the supreme pontiff that

---

15   This was Pierre A. Rost, not Alfred B. Rost.

the Northern armies were filled with soldiers of European birth, mostly from Ireland and the German states, and mostly Catholics. Lured by high bounties, they were, said Mann, "invariably placed in the most exposed points of danger in the battlefield" (that is, used as cannon fodder), and "that but for foreign recruits the North would have broken down months ago in the absurd attempt to overpower the South."[16] Upon hearing this, Pope Pius IX "expressed his utter astonishment ... at the employment of such means against us and the cruelty attendant upon such unscrupulous operations."[17]

Another purpose of Mann's mission to the Vatican was the delivery of a letter from President Jefferson Davis, who wished to thank Pope Pius IX for enjoining his archbishops at New York and New Orleans to offer prayers and use their influence for the restoration of peace in America. In his letter Davis assured the Pope that Southerners earnestly desired the war to end, that they wished no evil upon their enemies, and that they only desired the North to cease its hostilities and leave the South in peace. About a month later, Mann was given a letter for Davis written by Pope Pius IX. It was gracious response but not an official recognition of the Confederacy by the Vatican—yet Mann took it as such, as did others. Davis's biographer describes Mann's reaction to the papal reply and its consequences: "Mann took this to be recognition of the Confederacy: 'The hand of the Lord has been in it, and eternal glory and praise be to his holy and righteous name.' Judah Benjamin assured him that it was only a polite formula with no meaning because no diplomatic action followed. But the notion became widespread." [18]

As a diplomat, Mann was able, but he had his deficiencies, as well as his disagreements with Judah P. Benjamin, who served as the Confederate Secretary of War and then the Secretary of State. Mann's

---

16   The London newspaper *The Economist* reported that 180,000 Irish immigrated to America from 1861 to 1863, and that some 100,000 of these enlisted in the army of the United States; and that in 1864, over 60,000 Irish came to America, most of them joining the same army. *The Economist* also reported that "up to 1864 as many as 100,000 Germans had entered the northern army." Nearly all of these Germans were Catholics. Owsley, *King Cotton Diplomacy*, 497.

17   *A Compilation of the Messages and Papers of the Confederacy*, 594.

18   Allen, *Unconquerable Heart*, 441.

enthusiasm over the Pope's letter to Davis was just one example of his sometimes overly optimistic assessments of diplomatic affairs. John Preston Moore, who edited Mann's letters to Jefferson Davis, summed up his strengths and shortcomings as a diplomat thus: "He possessed industry, enthusiasm, and forthrightness, but he was unduly credulous and egotistical."[19]

Mann's efforts to obtain foreign recognition for his country failed, as did those of all the Confederate commissioners in Europe, but it is doubtful that any Southern representative could have succeeded in that daunting mission. In his book *The Glittering Illusion,* Sheldon Vanauken argues that, although the sympathies of the British were largely with the South during the war, their persistent belief that the South could not be defeated kept them from intervening in the conflict, or even offering recognition of the Confederacy. *The Times* of London, and all England, Vanauken maintained, "were in the grip of the glittering illusion, that Jefferson Davis *had made* a nation. Without England's having to risk a single warship, the end—desired as well as expected—of the disintegration of the American colossus and the establishment of a potential ally was virtually a *fait accompli.*"[20]

After other diplomatic visits to Paris, London, and elsewhere, Mann returned to Belgium and remained at that post until February 1865, when he was summoned to Paris to meet with Confederate commissioners Duncan F. Kenner, James Mason, and John Slidell. Kenner had just arrived on an urgent mission, having been instructed by the Confederate Secretary of State to seek the official recognition of Great Britain and France in exchange for the abolition of slavery in the Confederacy. After this meeting in Paris, Kenner and Mason went to London, where the latter obtained an interview with the Prime Minister, Lord Palmerston, on March 14, 1865. At this time, a bill had just passed in the Confederate Congress authorizing the

---

19 Mann, *"My Ever Dearest Friend,"* 23.
20 Vanauken, *The Glittering Illusion,* 133. Vanauken contended that England saw the South as aristocratic and thoroughly English, especially Virginia and the Carolinas.

arming of 300,000 slaves, but this measure, as well as Kenner's mission, would come too late, as the war ended in Southern defeat the following month.

In the spring, back in Brussels, Belgium, Mann learned of the collapse of the Confederacy, and the shock resulted in a physical breakdown. He wrote to Jefferson Davis that a physician had recommended that he take up residence in the region of Chantilly, France, and so he and his son purchased an estate there called Mont de Po.[21] Mann loved this beautiful country retreat, but the climate did not prove healthful for him in the winter, and he moved to Paris after an attack of asthma in November 1866. Mann continued to suffer periodically with asthma and gout, but in 1876 he apparently moved back to Mont de Po, which he began to call "Mon Repos" or "Mont Repos" and lived (or at least summered) there for several years thereafter.[22] In July 1878, hoping to entice Jefferson Davis to visit him, he described Mon Repos (variously spelled) in a letter to his dear friend:

> Now it is arrayed, with its surroundings, in its native beauty. A friend at Chantilly brought out a friend of his from Zurich, to introduce to me a few days ago. After surveying with his eyes the semi-circular panorama in front, the green little fields and the dozen villages beyond, the towering hills away off, in thick variegated verdant coiffed trees, he exclaimed, this is the most rural habitation that I have ever seen in France and is in favorable contrast as such with anything that Switzerland presents! Chantilly has become the centre of the gayest country region in France. The garden of Montrepos of few acres, is teeming with everything that the earth in this region produces, and as a miniature farm is well-nigh in perfection of

---

[21] According to a deed located by Daniel Frankignoul, Mont de Po was purchased in the name of William Grayson Mann. Frankignoul, Daniel. "A. Dudley Mann." Message to the editor, 7 March 2021. E-mail.

[22] Mann tried to sell Mont de Po more than once but was unsuccessful.

cultivation. The chasselas vines are loaded with grapes and the various fruit trees bending under the weight of their products. The yield of cherries, strawberries, raspberries is sufficient for a family of twenty persons. And I cannot omit to add that under the care of Marie[23] there are 150 or 160 spring chickens in the basse court, to say nothing of the large purebred stock which supply me with a superabundance of eggs, the most healthful and nourishing of all food.[24]

After the war, Mann obviously had enough financial resources to enable him to live at Chantilly and also rent an apartment in Paris, but it is not known how exactly how well he fared in terms of income in these or later years. He apparently supplemented it by writing.[25] A biographical sketch of Mann by Hubert Leroy of the Confederate Historical Association of Belgium states that he "worked as a journalist, sometimes signing his articles as "Colonel Mann."[26] In 1879 he informed Mrs. Keitt that some American investments he possessed, "securities in which I relied for perfect ease and independence," were now "next to worthless." Whatever his financial status might have been, he was welcome in the highest circles of French society. "In the French capital," Leroy noted, "he had entries to the closed circles of the aristocracy and other elitist salons. He was regarded as the senior of Americans living in Paris."[27]

In May of 1868, Mann had the pleasure of attending his son's wedding in Paris. Willie's first wife, Fannie Eliza Ogden Mann, a native of New Orleans, had died in France in 1864, and four years later he married Susie Cumming, the daughter of George B. Cumming,

---

23 Marie was Mann's housekeeper who worked for him for about twenty years.
24 Mann, *My Ever Dearest Friend,"* 64. A "basse-cour" is a kind of poultry yard.
25 Journalist Henry Watterson states in his autobiography that in the late 1850s Mann did editorial writing "incognito" for a Washington newspaper known as the *Daily Times*. Watterson, *"Marse Henry,"* 1:55. On June 22, 1859, a brief notice in the *Central City Courier* of Syracuse, N.Y., stated: "It is said that the Hon. Dudley Mann is to edit the Washington States." The *Washington States and Union* was a newspaper published in Washington, D.C.
26 Leroy, *Ambrose Dudley Mann*, 47.
27 Ibid.

a cotton merchant of Savannah, Georgia. A notice in a Charleston newspaper reported that the wedding of William Grayson Mann and "the beautiful Miss Cumming" was "attended by all the leading Southerners in Paris, including General Breckinridge and family, Mr. A. Dudley Mann, the father of the bridegroom, Judge John Perkins of Louisiana, &c., &c."[28] By March 1869, the newlyweds were living in Savannah, and made it their home for many years.

Mann continued to keep abreast of world events, and, while living in France, he had a firsthand knowledge of conditions and events in that country, witnessing the siege of Paris during the Franco-Prussian War of 1870-1871, and reporting many details in his letters to Mrs. Keitt. Mann was wholeheartedly on the side of the French, and quite confident of a French victory when the war began, but he would be proved wrong when the Prussians captured Paris in January 1871. During the siege, the city was heavily shelled, and there were severe shortages of food. Prussia's victory led to the unification of the German states, and Prussia's king, Wilhelm I, became the emperor of the German Empire as Kaiser Wilhelm. Humiliatingly enough for the French, his coronation took place at Versailles on January 18, 1871. Mann's antipathy for the Germans is evident in his letters. John Preston Moore surmised that his sojourn in the German states as a diplomat caused him to condemn their "illiberal political regime," but Mann had more reasons than this for his animus. He made the claim both to Mrs. Keitt and Jefferson Davis that the Confederacy would have won its independence but for German intervention, writing to the latter on August 24, 1870, that "Our poor fallen country would have maintained triumphantly its independence but for German arms and German money."[29] On July 20, 1870, he told Mrs. Keitt that "the aid which the North received from Germany in troops, money, etc." had led to the outcome of the war. A recent doctoral dissertation by David Thomson concerning the financing of the war documents how the United States government raised money for the war effort from the sale of bonds, many of which were purchased in Europe. The majority of these Union bonds were

---

28 *The Charleston Daily News,* May 27, 1868.
29 Davis, *The Papers of Jefferson Davis,* 12: 490.

sold in the German states, generating some 300 million dollars in investments, and this may account for some or all of the "German money" to which Mann was referring. Another work, *Germany and the Americas,* states that "Frankfurt bankers lent money to the U.S. government in the form of six large war bonds during the Civil War."

> Frankfurt achieved a key position in the financing of the American Civil War for two reasons: the efforts of the U.S. consul general, William Walton Murphy, and the influence of a group of Frankfurt's top bankers, which, over the years, had established a strong economic relationship with the United States.[30]

Mann was a Francophile, but not everything French was to his taste. As John Preston Moore pointed out, Mann "had an aversion to the dictatorship of Louis Napoleon."[31] He held a low opinion of the French emperor, and monarchies in general. Mrs. Keitt, on the other hand, was an admirer of Louis Napoleon (Napoleon III)—a difference of opinion for which the two correspondents made an "arrangement," agreeing to disagree amicably.

During the upheaval of the Franco-Prussian War, Louis Napoleon was overthrown, and the Third French Republic was established, with Adolphe Thiers as its first president. Not long after the war ended, Paris was taken over by a short-lived, quasi-revolutionary government known as the Paris Commune—a new city council made up of many different elements including neo-Jacobin republicans and anarchists. This mass takeover by the working class, which Karl Marx and Friedrich Engels idealized as the first "Dictatorship of the Proletariat," came to an end after only about two months, when the Communards were defeated by the regular French Army in the latter part of May 1871. Just after the Commune took over in March 1871, Mann began making plans to leave France (although later on he changed his mind and remained in his adopted country). He called the Communards the "Mob-Commune" and described them to Mrs.

---

30 Adam, *Germany and the Americas.* 61-62.
31 Mann, *"My Ever Dearest Friend,"* 23.

Keitt in his letter of June 1, 1871, as "the largest, best organized, and most desperate, body of robbers and assassins, that ever leagued together. It was composed of the evil spirits of every land. The Yankees were not without fit representation in it. Its paramount object was pillage, at whatever sacrifice of life to the pillaged." There were many Americans in Paris at this time, and among those who joined with the Communards were men who had fought for the North during the recent war between the United States and the Confederate States. Other Communards included Gustave Paul Cluseret and Regis de Trobriand, French natives who had served as high-ranking officers in the Union Army.

It is not well known that in 1872, Mann published a book under the pen name "Tuckahoe."[32] It was entitled *The Life of Tammie Chattie of Le Bosquet des Rossignols, Victim of the Siege of Paris.*[33] Advertisements that appeared at the time of its publication by Ward, Lock, and Tyler of London described it as "The work of a diplomatist known on both sides of the Atlantic, and long resident in Paris" whose writing revealed "a pleasant and amiable disposition." This quaint, often charming novella is principally the story of how Mann acquired three beloved pets at Mont de Po—Tammie Chattie, an Angora cat, Bizzie, a Scottish terrier, and Stentor, a Newfoundland dog. In his letter of March 1867 to Mrs. Keitt, Mann wrote affectionately of these three pets. Chapter seventeen of the novella recounts how Tammie Chattie became a "victim" of the siege of Paris when he disappeared one day on a mousing expedition, and the book ends with a lament over this loss which is quoted from one of Jefferson Davis's letters to Mann.[34] The famine caused by the Prussian siege forced Parisians to eat rats, cats, and other animals (including elephants from the zoo),

---

32   "Tuckahoe" was a term that referred to low country, planter class Virginians. Tuckahoe Plantation in Virginia was the boyhood home of Thomas Jefferson. Mann apparently used this pseudonym more than once. In January 1871, he sent by balloon mail, "a copy of his broadside signed 'Tuckahoe' and addressed to King William I of Prussia." Davis, *The Papers of Jefferson Davis,* 13:3.

33   The full name of Mann's Chantilly farm was Bosquet des Rossignols a Mont de Po. The first part of the name means "Grove of Nightingales."

34   "'Poor Tammie!' he remarked, 'more faithful than many who have a future life, was cut off in all his wealth of loveliness without the compensation given to man.'" Tuckahoe, *The Life of Tammie Chattie,* 117. The quote is from a letter from Davis to Mann dated July 15, 1871, found in volume 13 of *The Papers of Jefferson Davis* (48).

and Mann had told Davis that his cat "fell a victim on the 103rd day of the siege to a voracious human, or rather inhuman, appetite."[35] As it turned out, however, the cat actually survived and eventually returned to Mann at some point. In May 1879 he wrote to Mrs. Keitt that "Tammie Chattie" was still with him and that he had no time to write a sequel to his story.

Mann's letters to Mrs. Keitt document two visits by ex-Confederate President Jefferson Davis, the first of which occurred in the winter of 1868-1869. Davis was accompanied by his wife Varina, and Mann proudly reported to Mrs. Keitt that the French people "were entirely captivated with him." Mann tried to convince his old friend to settle in France, but he was too attached to his beloved South. The pure-minded Davis was also put off by the worldliness of Paris, although he did return there for a second time in the summer of 1874, staying with Mann for a month. On these two occasions Davis went abroad mainly for reasons of health, and his first trip included tours of Liverpool and Edinburgh, but, financially ruined, he also sought business opportunities in England and France. He had been cruelly imprisoned for two years after the war, awaiting a trial for treason that never took place. The legal case against Davis was not dropped until February 1869, so he was still under its cloud during his first visit to Paris, during which Mann praised him as "a magnificent representation of Majesty in adversity." Davis would visit Mann in Paris again in 1876, and in 1881, he spent some time with his friend at his country home in Chantilly.[36]

Mann urged Mrs. Keitt many times to leave the South, partly because of the deplorable conditions there after the war. "Come to me," he entreated, and his letters indicate that at least twice, she gave him to understand that she would do that. "Be happy; I will come," Mann wrote rapturously, quoting from one of her letters—but sadly, as far as we know, he would only see her face again when they

---

35 Davis, *The Papers of Jefferson Davis*, 13:19.
36 In 1881, Varina Davis wrote to her daughter that Mann was "the most generous & refined of gentlemen, and one who loves your Father better than his life, he is inexpressibly dear to us & has been for thirty years." Allen, *Unconquerable Heart*, 546.

exchanged photographs. She asked him to come and visit her, but he had sworn a "sacred" vow that he would never return to America unless he returned to an independent South.

Ambrose Dudley Mann lived to the ripe old age of 88, passing away on November 15, 1889. According to an obituary that appeared in the *New-York Tribune* on December 1, 1889, his funeral services were held in Paris at the American Cathedral of the Holy Trinity on the Avenue de l'Alma. For many decades the location of his grave was unknown, but in 2008, Hubert Leroy succeeded in finding it in the cemetery of Montparnasse in Paris. Neglected for more than a hundred years, the stone sarcophagus was covered with dirt and moss, and Leroy and other members of the Confederate Historical Association of Belgium cleaned it to reveal the inscriptions.

Mann's epitaph is a verse from the Beatitudes: "Blessed are the pure in heart."

SUSANNA MANDEVILLE SPARKS KEITT

Born in 1834, Sue Sparks Keitt was the daughter of Samuel Sparks and his second wife Ann Harry Sparks. He was a wealthy Marlboro District planter who owned a large plantation called Mandeville, and a summer resort property called Mineral Springs.[37] Sue's paternal ancestors, descendants of James Sparks of Virginia, moved into the Pee Dee region of South Carolina and settled in Welsh Neck, an area along the Pee Dee River in Marlboro District (now Marlboro County). Sue's grandfather, Captain David Sparks, had commanded a company of South Carolina militia troops during the Revolution.

---

37 "Several wealthy planters who owned plantations near the [Pee Dee] river, built summer houses at Mineral Spring, or Spring Hill (called by both names), where they resided during the summer months. It being unhealthy on the river in the summer, they annually moved out to the Spring for the double purpose of finding a healthy locality and good cold water." Thomas, *A History of Marlboro County,* 191. The area developed into the town of Blenheim.

Sue grew up to be a beautiful young woman. She was also exceptionally intelligent, and part of her education included studies at Barhamville Academy, where she developed an interest in music and art. The formal name for this school, which was located near Columbia, S.C., was the South Carolina Female Collegiate Institute. Sue's father was one of its patrons.

In 1854, Sue met Laurence Massillon Keitt. A native of Orangeburg District, S.C., and a graduate of South Carolina College, he was admitted to the bar in 1845 and began a law practice in the town of Orangeburg. Keitt served two terms in the state legislature, and in 1852 he was elected to the United States Congress, where he remained until he withdrew to become a delegate to the Secession Convention of his state in 1860. Keitt was a "longtime supporter of states' rights, even to the extent of South Carolina seceding alone," and his views on government coincided closely with those of Ambrose Dudley Mann.[38]

> Intense individualism and devotion to Jeffersonian principles of simplicity in government made him an independent Democrat, 'a Constitutional Democrat,' as he called himself ... Keitt was well versed in the classics, contemporary history, and economic philosophy, and he had the firm religious faith of the orthodox South. Though sometimes bombastic, his lengthy speeches were a great force, telling in phrase, and eloquent with burning conviction ... Keitt's dashing appearance and forceful delivery attracted the attention of the northern press and won him many invitations to speak in northern states, where his favorite topics were the defense of slavery, the acquisition of Cuba, and the part played by South Carolina in the Revolutionary War.[39]

---
38 Sifakis, *Who Was Who in the Civil War,* 357.
39 Culler, *Orangeburgh District,* 316.

In 1855, Keitt proposed to Sue, but many weeks passed before she accepted, and thereafter she postponed or called off the wedding several times. It was not until September 1858 that the engagement was on again. They were finally married in May 1859, after which they left the country for a European tour. Sue wished to stay abroad indefinitely, but their European honeymoon was cut short in October 1859 when political tensions at home began to boil over and Keitt decided that he must return to Congress. John Brown's murderous raid in Virginia had deepened the sectional rift between North and South, and made Southerners feel more anxious about their safety in the Union.[40] Historian Nathaniel Wright Stephenson pointed out that it is "almost impossible today to realize the state of the country" at that time. "The bad feeling between the two sections, all came to a head, and burst into fury, over the episode of John Brown."[41]

In December 1859 the Keitts took up residence in Washington, D.C. At first Sue did not care for Washington society, and was rather alarmed by the vitriolic rhetoric exchanged by political factions, but she grew more interested in politics (and more ambitious on behalf of her husband), and before long she became caught up in the whirl of the city's social life. She charmed President James Buchanan and many other prominent people, and her admirer Ambrose Dudley Mann would become a close friend and confidante.[42]

In her memoir *A Belle of the Fifties,* Virginia Clay-Clopton wrote of Sue: "Mrs. Keitt was one of Washington's most admired young matrons, a graceful hostess, and famous for her social enterprise. It was she who introduced in the capital the fashion of sending out birth-cards to announce the arrival of infants."[43] Sue must have sent out one of these cards when her first child, Anna, was born in May

---

[40] John Brown unsuccessfully attempted to capture weapons at an armory at Harper's Ferry and lead an armed slave rebellion. It soon became known that his raid had been funded by six prominent Northern abolitionists, and after his execution many abolitionists and literati in the North glorified him as a martyr. Newspaper reports described Brown's maps of Southern states (including South Carolina) which were ominously marked to indicate the locations of more plotted uprisings.

[41] Stephenson, *An American History,* 401.

[42] Mrs. Keitt's relationship with President Buchanan is explored in John Updike's play *Buchanan Dying*. Her husband Laurence Massillon Keitt is also a character in the play.

[43] Clay-Clopton, *A Belle of the Fifties,* 96.

1860, but the occasion was not wholly joyous, as the new mother fell ill, and in August the Keitts took up residence at a South Carolina health resort, Glenn Springs, where she recovered.

Keitt resigned his seat in the U.S. House of Representatives a few days before the South Carolina Secession Convention began in December 1860, and on the 20th of that month, the state seceded and declared itself "an independent Commonwealth." Other Southern states followed, and in February 1861, in Montgomery, Alabama, they formed the Confederate States of America. Keitt became a member of the Provisional Confederate Congress. He was highly displeased when Jefferson Davis was elected as the Confederate president; unlike Ambrose Dudley Mann, Keitt considered Davis "a failure, and his cabinet a farce."[44] As a politician, Keitt was prominent among the so-called fire-eaters, who were outspoken advocates of an independent South. The derogatory term "fire-eater" seems to have originated in Northern newspapers, and some historians have held these Southern politicians responsible for fomenting secession and war, but the fire-eaters themselves considered that their states had been forced into secession for self-preservation.[45] Keitt did not believe that Southern secession would result in "coercion on the part of the North," but of course the North did choose to respond to secession with force.[46] After serving in the Confederate Congress for about a year, he entered military service as a colonel of the 20th South Carolina Infantry Regiment, which served in the defense of Charleston and later in Virginia.

For many months in 1861, Sue and her infant daughter stayed at her father's plantation, Mandeville, and it was from this place she penned an interesting letter to a Northern friend, Mrs. Frederick Brown, whom she had met on her European honeymoon. Writing about a month before the war began, Sue set forth some of her

---

[44] Chesnut, *A Diary from Dixie,* 65.
[45] "Southern belief in a Northern determination to transform the United States into a consolidated nation, where the majority must always rule a central government endowed with large, indefinite implied powers, loomed as a grave threat to many Southerners' most cherished ideals of society, of government, of life itself. Johnson, *North Against South,* 74.
[46] *Charleston Courier,* Nov. 21, 1860, 4.

views on the reasons for the South's withdrawal from the union as the threat of war loomed. "All we have done," she explained, "is to withdraw from the Union when it fails to guarantee our safety."[47] In December 1861, Sue's second daughter, Stella, was born.

Col. Keitt spent over two years in the Charleston area, mostly as a commander of forces on Sullivan's Island. Sue was also in Charleston or nearby for much of that time. From August 1863 onward, the city was under bombardment from Federal artillery on Morris Island. In her husband's papers at Duke University, there is a letter she wrote to Ambrose Dudley Mann in the spring of 1864. At the time it was composed, she was staying in a safer location across the Cooper River in Mount Pleasant.[48] This eloquent letter is addressed to "Hon. A. Dudley Mann" in Paris, and she greets him as "My dear and honored friend." It is likely a copy of a letter that she sent out of Charleston via a blockade runner. In it, she describes the enemy's siege of the city, which was the longest of the war.

In the latter part of May 1864, Col. Keitt's regiment was ordered to Virginia, and only two weeks later, at the Battle of Cold Harbor, he was mortally wounded, and died the next day.[49] His grave is in St. Matthews, S.C., a town near his plantation home, Puritan Farm.[50]

In 1865, Sue and her two daughters were again living at Mandeville with her parents. During the winter of that year, the army of General William T. Sherman was moving through South Carolina, cutting a wide path of destruction across the state, burning and looting farms, plantations and towns; demolishing railroads; destroying or confiscating crops and livestock; and plundering and abusing civilians. On March 6, 1865, Sherman's XVII Corps occupied

---

47 Herd, "Sue Sparks Keitt," 85.
48 Merchant, *South Carolina Fire-Eater*, 188.
49 Like Ambrose Dudley Mann, Laurence M. Keitt had an "almost idolatrous love" for Sue Keitt. In the afterword to his play *Buchanan Dying*, John Updike noted: "The Keitt correspondence, at Duke University, is fascinating, as history, and as the record of a great love; an edited publication would, if not surpass the correspondence of Heloise and Abelard, provide an American variant." *Buchanan Dying*, 230. Keitt's last words were: "Oh, wife. Wife."
50 The town of St. Matthews is in Calhoun County, which was created in 1908 from the South Carolina counties of Orangeburg and Lexington.

Bennettsville, a town not far from Mandeville Plantation. A Union soldier recorded in his diary that they found the town nearly deserted because "many [South Carolina] citizens hid in the swamps, some with their children. They have heard such terrible tales of our cruelty to the people in our line of march."[51] When Sherman's soldiers began raiding surrounding areas in Marlboro District, they did not fail to pay a visit to Mandeville, where they ransacked and pillaged the house and the plantation for hours and demanded whiskey from Sue's mother, Mrs. Sparks, who had none.[52]

Little is known of Sue's activities in the early postwar years, except that in October 1865 she wrote to Benjamin F. Perry, the provisional governor of South Carolina, begging him to help her save her plantation property without swearing the hated oath of allegiance to the United States.[53] Perry could offer her no help, however, and eventually Sue must have given in and taken the oath, since she retained the Keitt plantation in Orangeburg District.[54] The following year—as if widowhood, defeat in war, and impoverishment were not enough misfortunes to bear—she also lost her youngest daughter Stella, who died on February 18, 1866. After this Sue must have been thinking of her own mortality, and, concerned about what might happen to her other child, she asked Mann if he would agree to be Anna's guardian. She may have considered that Anna would be better off under his care in France rather than living with family members in the devastated South. It is not clear whether this was a formal or informal arrangement, but he proudly accepted the responsibility.

Mann's letters to Mrs. Keitt begin in January 1867, and the first three are addressed to her in Charleston. From February 1868 until early June 1871, they are addressed to her in Charleston care

---

51 Anderson, *The Civil War Diary of Allen Morgan Geer*, 202.
52 Rutledge, "Elizabeth Jamison's Tale of the War," 32.
53 South Carolinian Emma LeConte wrote in her diary in May 1865: "They are administering the oath here now and almost everyone is obliged to take it for unless they do they are not allowed to engage in any occupation, nor to travel beyond the limits of the town, nor will they be protected against violence or injustice of any kind." LeConte, *When the World Ended*, 107.
54 Merchant, *South Carolina Fire-Eater*, 193-194.

of Williams Middleton, who owned a fine house in the city as well as nearby Middleton Place, a magnificent rice plantation on the Ashley River. Mann refers to Sue's place of residence as a "delightful little locale," which does not make it clear whether she was staying at Middleton's townhouse or his plantation, or possibly some other "locale" in the Charleston area.[55] The letters are also unclear on her relationship with Williams Middleton, but he and Sue's husband (both signers of South Carolina's Ordinance of Secession) knew each other, and may have been good friends. Sue also had a family connection to the Middletons. Her first cousin, Dr. William Alexander Sparks, married Alicia Middleton, the daughter of John Middleton, who was a cousin of Williams Middleton.[56] From late June 1871 onward, Mann directed his most of his letters to her at Bennettsville, S.C.

In a letter of May 1871, Mann remarked on "pair of admirers" who were courting Mrs. Keitt, asking, "Do they still woo without hope?" No clue is given to their identity, but they were indeed hopeless. She never remarried.

When Sue's father died in 1878, his estate was heavily in debt, and Mandeville was put up for auction to pay off the creditors.[57] Intent on saving her family land, she borrowed money from a local merchant. He exacted high interest rates on more than one loan, and her dealings with him involved many setbacks, contentions, and difficulties. Once, when she missed a mortgage payment, she declared she would enter a convent if he did not give her more time to raise the money—but this was not the first time Sue had contemplated monastic life. In 1871 she had written to Mann about

---

[55] Middleton Place, like nearly every other plantation along the Ashley River, was looted and burned by Federal forces in 1865 after the occupation of Charleston. One wing of Williams Middleton's beautiful mansion house which was left standing was later repaired and rebuilt to create the house there now. Writing just after World War I, historian Henry A. M. Smith noted of the fate of the Ashley River plantations: "The whole scene of destruction was as complete as that of the French Chateaux rifled, despoiled, and burnt by the German army in Northern France." Stokes, *Confederate South Carolina*, 126.

[56] Dr. Sparks died in 1849 and his widow later married General Roswell S. Ripley.

[57] A plantation near St. Matthew's belonging to Anna Keitt was also mortgaged sometime after the war.

her "notion of going with dear Anna to a Convent, and becoming an Instructress therein." He was appalled by the idea, ascribing it to her discouragement and depression, and it distressed him that he was not able to help her financially. In 1879, the house at Mandeville was destroyed in a fire, and Mann commiserated with her in the loss of her "old historical mansion."

Eventually, Sue managed to repay the loans, and she restored the family plantation lands to prosperity, so much so that she became moderately wealthy in her later years, and was able to provide well for Anna, sending her to Augusta Female College in Virginia. In Sue's later years, she and her daughter traveled extensively in Europe and other foreign locales.

The last surviving communication between Mann and Mrs. Keitt is a Christmas greeting jotted on his calling card in 1882. The brief message indicates that she has not written to him since June of that year, and he expresses his longing to hear from her, but it is not known whether they continued to correspond, or ever saw each other again. If any of Sue's foreign travels took place before Ambrose Dudley Mann's death in 1889, it is possible that she and Anna may have paid him a visit him in France, thus granting him his "most desired of all earthly joys."

Sue died "at her country home near Bennettsville" on January 21, 1915.[58] One of her obituaries states that she was "active up to within a short while of her death" and that she and her daughter were in Wiesbaden, Germany, when the World War began in 1914.[59] According to her death certificate, the primary cause of death was listed as pleurisy, and secondarily, as pneumonia. She was buried at the West End Cemetery in Saint Matthews, S.C., where her husband also rests. Anna Keitt never married. She died in New York City in 1919 and was buried in the same cemetery as her parents.

---

58 *The State,* January 24, 1915, 3.
59 *The State,* January 22, 1915, 3.

Introduction

The Letters

Ambrose Dudley Mann's letters touch on many subjects, including other ex-Confederates in France, politics in South Carolina and the United States as a whole, conditions in Paris during the Franco-Prussian War, and the writing of his memoirs, but his principal theme is his ardent love for Mrs. Keitt, and his concern for her and her daughter Anna. His confident belief that Mrs. Keitt valued him, and his friendship, was the "pride and glory" of his life. In return, he gave her "a love as holy as high, as pure, as constant as ever animated in human heart—not the love of mortal passion but the love of Celestial bliss." He called himself her lover, representing his feelings for her as a reverent, Platonic love, and yet in more than one letter, when speculating about seeing her in person, he confessed his fear that the nature of his love might change. "Although so many years your senior," he wrote to her in June 1871, "I fear to trust myself in the presence of your captivating person, lest it may assume a different character." He was seventy years old at the time, and Mrs. Keitt was thirty-seven.

She was his ideal of womanhood, and he not only admired her beauty but also her intelligence, culture, and independent spirit, writing to her with a poignant yearning that never seemed to fade. Mann often praised her in the most exalted terms, and went into ecstasies over the photographs of herself that she sent to him.

Mann's other earthly idol was the South, especially its incarnation as an independent confederacy founded on the republican principles he revered. In March 1871 he wrote to Mrs. Keitt that "A Republic, such as was Virginia and South-Carolina in other days, and such as Switzerland is at present, is the best form of Government ever given to mankind." Later, in June 1871, he declared, "I intend to die, as I have lived, a moderate Republican such as was Washington, Jefferson, Calhoun and the glorious men of the South of their times."

He could never accept the destruction of his beloved Confederacy, and among the Southern "irreconcilables" he may have been the most adamant. He had nothing but loathing for the Northerners who had brought about that destruction— a sentiment he held in common with Mrs. Keitt, telling her in one of his early letters, "There is but one female in existence, with whom I am personally acquainted, who shares my sentiments of unmitigated hate to Northerners." Mann did not hold a high opinion of the statesmanship of Judah P. Benjamin, his former superior in the Confederate State Department, but he would have fully concurred with Benjamin's assessment of "Yankees," who, during the war, "could not help showing their cruelty and rapacity; they could not dissemble their true nature, which is the real cause of this war."[60]

Although forced back into the Union by military defeat, many Southerners never accepted the outcome of the war—a war which, like Mann, they viewed as unnecessary and unjust, and further, they bitterly resented the way it had been waged. Mrs. Keitt's home state had been ravaged by the army of General Sherman, and Georgia and other states also suffered at his hands. Especially in Georgia and South Carolina, his was a policy of total war which involved aggressions against noncombatants—and Sherman was not its only practitioner. It was no wonder that so many Southerners shared Mann's and Keitt's passionate feelings about the North. "The acts of terror committed against the civilian populace of the South by Sherman's troops," wrote one of Sherman's biographers, "indeed planted seeds of hatred that bore bitter fruit and postponed a sense of unity and understanding between the people of the United States far longer than might otherwise have been the case."[61]

In a letter to a lawyer in South Carolina, General John Smith Preston, one of Mann's fellow Confederate expatriates in Paris, bitterly lamented that he would someday have to return to his home state:

> "I go back with the gloomiest anticipations, both as to my own affairs and the general condition of the country. Were I able to live out of it I would never put my foot on the soil again ever although all other

---
60 Ross, *Cities and Camps of the Confederate States*, 24.
61 Walters, *Merchant of Terror*, 207.

places are of deathly meanness to me, none more so than this glittering Paris. But I regard South Carolina at an end, all gone, not a grease spot left ... A rapid wasting away under our fruitless struggles is all that we are allowed to hope. Already you are not the equal of the negro. And you are the slave of the Yankee."[62]

Many events that occurred in the period following the war only deepened Southern hostility toward the North. Lincoln's successor, President Andrew Johnson, believed in a moderate, conciliatory policy in dealing with the former Confederate states, but the vindictive Radical Republicans in Washington opposed his policies and sought to impose harsh measures on the South. One of the most virulent of the radicals was Thaddeus Stevens, a powerful Congressman from Pennsylvania. "According to his creed, the insurgent states were conquered provinces to be shaped into a paradise for the freedmen and a hell for the rebel."[63] The former states of the Confederacy were put under military rule for a period, and during the second phase of Reconstruction ("Congressional Reconstruction") the new state governments in the South were put in place and controlled by Republican coalitions which were sometimes corrupt and oppressive.

> Aside from the unforgiveable sin of being controlled by an unholy alliance of carpetbaggers, scalawags, and blacks, Republican governments were most often criticized for imposing crushing taxes on the mass of whites so as to raise money for graft and extravagances.[64]

In Mrs. Keitt's native state, the carpetbagger regime "was responsible for stealing millions of dollars from the citizens of South Carolina by perpetrating all types of financial scams."[65] Historian

---

62 John S. Preston to James Simons, November 1, 1866. John S. Preston Correspondence.
63 Dewitt, *The Impeachment and Trial of Andrew Johnson*, 27.
64 Johnson, *North Against South*, 248.
65 Shull, *A Guide Book of Southern States Currency*, 297.

William B. Hesseltine wrote of the corruption and election fraud in South Carolina after the Republican state government was installed, noting how fourteen regiments of black militia "terrorized the wavering blacks and prevented whites from voting. In one electoral campaign, the militia cost the State $374,000."

> The State owned stock in the Columbia and Greenville Railroad which was lost through the mismanagement of the radical manager. The Blue Ridge Railroad had $2,000,000 of its scrip endorsed by the State and receivable for taxes.
>
> Extensive graft occurred with the refurnishing of the State House. Elaborate furnishings replaced—at exorbitant cost—the simple fixtures of a former day ... Favors were procured from the legislature by bribery and a Congressman sold a West Point appointment ... A grandiose scheme for purchasing land for distribution to the Negroes resulted in the expenditure of almost $800,000, of which $225,000 was graft for the commission. In the end, the State came into possession of thousands of acres of worn-out and infertile land ... Under the radical regime, the State debt increased from less than $6,000,000 to more than $25,000,000.[66]

The corruption evident in postwar American politics in both the North and South (especially during President Grant's second term) disgusted Mann, and he was ashamed of "scalawag" Southerners who cooperated with Republicans in Washington and the carpetbagger governments in the states. In 1873 he wrote to Jefferson Davis that "the North is in steady if not rapid consummation of ruin of the Federal System."[67]

---

66   Hesseltine, *A History of the South,* 628-29.
67   Mann, *"My Ever Dearest Friend,"* 36.

INTRODUCTION

Mrs. Keitt often wrote to Mann about conditions in South Carolina and the South in general during and after Reconstruction. He also kept himself informed of American events through newspaper reports. In 1868 he followed the impeachment proceedings against President Andrew Johnson. When he learned that Johnson was acquitted, Mann predicted that there would be division among the Republicans, and that efforts to enact "Negro suffrage" would fail because of it. Mann did not favor social equality and voting rights for the former slaves, but in the nineteenth century, the vast majority of white Americans, North and South, held the same views, and regarded blacks as an inferior people. Historian Ludwell H. Johnson noted that in the state elections of 1867, Negro suffrage was put to the voters in three Northern states and rejected by all three.[68] By 1870, when the 15th Amendment to the Constitution gave the vote to black men, only seven states in the North had already voluntarily done so.[69] Johnson explained that as early as the spring of 1865, "influential Republicans had concluded that Negro suffrage would eventually be required to entrench their party in power, although they approached the subject very cautiously to avoid antagonizing anti-Negro northern voters."[70]

Mann was not only dismayed by the political and social trends he saw in America, but also in Europe. He was horrified by the socialist "Mob-Commune" takeover in Paris, and as the years went on, he observed the progress of Marxist ideology in Europe with alarm. On New Year's Day in 1884, he penned a letter to Jefferson Davis, musing pessimistically about the march of Western civilization in Europe toward nihilism, socialism, and communism. The United States, he contended, was marching not far behind in the same direction, and that unfortunately, the only force which could have checked that progress, at least in America, was the South—but a South now gone. He wrote to his old friend:

---

68   Johnson. *North Against South*, 232.
69   *Ibid.*, 243.
70   *Ibid.* 195.

I never was more bothered in mind for the formation of an opinion as to what point of descent the, so denominated civilized world is wending as on this New Year's morning; nor do I believe that the brightest human vision can foresee. The propitious progress which it is making downward, in general demoralization, forbids a rational expectation that a halt is probable. Vice is in such supreme role everywhere that the masses of humankind are disgusted with government and are steadily embracing the sentiment of nihilism. Anarchy has become the impelling motive of their thoughts. Universal suffrage will not satisfy them. The potentates of Europe fancy that it will. Even Bismarck counts upon it as a cure for the Socialism of Germany. Gladstone seems to be quite willing to enlarge the elective franchise in Great Britain but he is met with the extremely puzzling question, to what extent? In like manner all the other premiers of the monarchs of Europe are secretly embarrassed for a trustworthy solution. But each, in the supposed interest of his reigning Mistress or Master, has no alternative but to make a 'merit of necessity' and allow every citizen to vote—and that before the lapse of a lengthened period. The political power thus created will inevitably sweep away the existing thrones. But it will not be inclined to stop with this procedure. It will institute Communism and precipitate a general division of property. The vox populi of the United States will not be far behind the lead of the movement. There was that virtue once in the South that would have efficiently checked such an attempt, but it has, as I contemplate the matter, actively disappeared. The sensibility of principle, in the control of affairs, no longer exists in that former Heaven favored land.[71]

---

71 Mann, *"My Ever Dearest Friend,"* 88-89.

Mann was working on his memoirs as early as May 1867, when he informed Mrs. Keitt that he had enough material "to fill many volumes." In February 1868, he told her that he was "almost constantly occupied" with his book, which would consist of three volumes written for posterity, and "in the interests of truthful history." In May 1879, in his last full letter to Mrs. Keitt, Mann reported that he was still working on his book. At some point he decided to expand or divide it into four and then five parts, writing to Jefferson Davis in late 1882 that the fourth volume was "dedicated exclusively to the diplomacy of the Confederate States in Europe, which will take the intelligent world of readers by surprise."[72]

When his memoir was finally completed, Mann handed it over to his son, along with other papers, including letters.[73] According to a newspaper article, Mann instructed his son Willie that his memoirs must not be published until six years after his death. This article, published in a Savannah newspaper on August 16, 1896, also stated that "Judge Mann" (William Grayson Mann) was editing his father's papers and preparing them for publication, however, Judge Mann passed away later that year in Chicago on November 20, and it has never been determined what happened to the papers of his father; they were certainly never published.[74] Strangely enough, an obituary for William Grayson Mann that appeared in another newspaper stated: "During the last years of his life Judge Mann was engaged in writing his father's memoirs, which were published recently."[75]

In 1901, the following inquiry by "L.L.K." appeared in the English journal *Notes and Queries*: "Ambrose Dudley Mann, the diplomatist, has written his 'Memoirs,' which were in 1888 ready

---

72 *Ibid.*, 78.
73 Many of Mann's letters have survived in collections of official correspondence, as well as in the papers of his correspondents, such as Jefferson Davis and James M. Mason.
74 William Grayson Mann's will was filed in Chicago, and his third wife, Minerva Myers Mann, was his principal heir and an executrix of his estate. They apparently had no children. In 1897 she petitioned the Cook County Probate Court to sell off various real estate properties belonging to the estate to pay its creditors. Mrs. Mann died in New York City in 1907 at the age of 55 and is buried in Cincinnati, Ohio.
75 *Stevens Point Journal* (Wisconsin), November 23, 1896, 2.

for publication, according to Appleton's 'Encylcopaedia of American Biography.' Have they been published; and if not, what has become of the MS.?"[76]

This last question has never been answered.

---

[76] *Notes and Queries,* 329.

Ambrose Dudley Mann's Letters to Mrs. Keitt, 1867-1879

Ambrose Dudley Mann, Paris, France, to Mrs. Sue Sparks Keitt, c/o John Fraser & Company, Charleston, S.C.

27 January 1867

My Ever Dear and Good Friend:

A suspension of four months in your correspondence occasions me a large amount of additional anxiety for your well-being. Fears flit across my mind that your health may not be good, or that you may be otherwise afflicted.

Upon the receipt of your last beautiful Letter I wrote to you at considerable length, and a week thereafter I wrote again; and as I have not received an acknowledgment of either I fear that neither reached its destination.

In November I had a new and terrific attack of the Chest disease which prostrated me in August and as soon as I was sufficiently recovered to walk across to my chamber my Physician urged me to quit Mont Po[77] for the winter. He thought that the climate of this City would relieve if not restore me; but if it failed to do so I must repair to Nice. Gen. Breckinridge[78] came out and bore me off. It was a struggle for me to quit, even temporarily, my sweet chosen retreat— the endeared home of my adoption. But the pure air which rendered it so healthful nine months of the year was too fierce for sensitive lungs during the cold season. I am at last completely restored, as free from a distressful cough as I was before I was attacked. It is only recently that I was permitted to sit at my desk.

---

77 Mont Po was Mann's country home in Chantilly, France. In one of his letters he refers to it as the Chateau of Mont Po. It was located near the Chateau de Chantilly, which is now an historic monument open to the public. In a letter to Jefferson Davis, Mann wrote that his spacious country house was on six acres of land enclosed with stone walls. *Papers of Jefferson Davis,* 323.

78 John Breckenridge (1821-1875) was the Vice President of the United States under James Buchanan, and during the War Between the States he served in the Confederate Army as a general and later as the Confederate Secretary of War. Breckenridge's visit to France was just one of the many stops on his tour of Europe during his exile between 1865-1868.

I hope, with all my heart, that you are more <u>sans souci</u> than when you last wrote. Now that I am so well I often think what an enjoyment it would be to me if I could be favored with your society. There are many Southerners here, some of them very refined and intelligent, but none in whom I take so much interest as I do in yourself and dear little Anna. Of the <u>true</u> to that cause which is so consecrated in my affections I esteem you as the <u>most true</u> ever of your devoted sex. If there were no ties of the past to bind you and your darling [inexorably] to me this would, alone, be a sufficient one. I love the faithful in adversity with a love which I fancy is inspired by Him who so peculiarly loved the "faithful disciple."

I am in daily communication with all the Confederates who are here, (and they are very numerous) and listen to all they have to say—ladies as well as gentlemen—but alas! I find but few who are not ready to go over to the enemy. I grieve the more for my fallen country—for the nobles slain in battle—when I see the willingness with which their sons and daughters identify themselves with the Yankees. I stand almost alone in unyielding resistance to their insidious indirect advances. There is but one female in existence, with whom I am personally acquainted, who shares my sentiments of unmitigated hate to Northerners—your excellent self. I need not beseech you to continue in your faith; I know that it is as unshakeable as the "Rock of Ages," because it is founded in <u>eternal</u> [principle].

Anarchy seems inevitable in the North. I cannot perceive any manner in which it can be escaped. The Impeachment of Johnson will precipitate the event. Whether he resists or not the result will be the same. The Constitution is already, to all intents and purposes, a dead letter.

I have been constantly on the <u>qui vive</u> for a suitable French instructress for dear little Anna. I have not, however, succeeded in finding a suitable one in all respects. The most competent are unwilling to leave France, for they find ample employment at high wages. After the World's Fair[79] they may be in less demand. I so

---

[79] The Exposition Universelle (international exposition) took place in Paris from April 1 to November 3, 1867.

much wish that you were both here. Nothing could afford me so much pleasure as to take her little hand in mine and conduct her, in my daily walks, to witness the thousands of objects that would amuse and instruct her.

Direct your Letters as usual to Chantilly, and write I pray you My dear Mrs. Keitt, as frequently as your convenience will permit.

Ever and Devotedly Your Friend,

   A. Dudley Mann

Ambrose Dudley Mann, Paris, to Mrs. Sue Sparks Keitt, Charleston, S.C., c/o John Fraser & Co.

28 March 1867

My Ever Dear and Excellent Friend:

I wrote, under date of 3rd and 8th last (acknowledging the receipt of your Letter commenced at Charleston and finished at Mandeville) three closely covered sheets, which I trust reached you safely.

The fresh calamity, resulting from fiendish legislation, added to her other enormous humiliations, is more than the South can support, and I fear that you are in great distress of mind.[80] Envy has ever been foreign to my nature, and yet I almost envy those noble spirits who fell in the midst of battle, in defense of our glorious cause. I wish I had been in the thickest of the fight and gone down by their side. I should have been spared the agony of heart which now afflicts me, in beholding ever from afar my beloved country in worse bondage than ever was exercised by any nation upon its victim. What the end is to be of the demon-like rule of Congress the Almighty alone knows. Oh! that you and your darling Anna were here in France. I am anxious, most anxious, for you both; for I fear under cruel Military Rule woe may betide you. In this smiling, joyous land you would be as secure as you would be free; and during my life you would find in me a protector and friend, in whom you could implicitly confide. Do, do come, and come quickly, if there be not insurmountable barriers to your departure.

I am now preparing to return to my dear home—to my flowers, my vines, my orchards, my vegetable garden, and the other sweet associations of rural life and romantic scenery. The first notes of the Nightingale will serenade my arrival. The Lark, with the dew on his breast, will greet at the early dawn my coming. And the thousand

---

80 The first Reconstruction acts were passed by the U.S. Congress in March 1867. Among other things, they established five military districts in the South under the control of powerful generals, required the former Confederate states to ratify the Fourteenth Amendment, and also required new state constitutions. President Andrew Johnson considered these acts unconstitutional and vetoed them, but Congress overrode his vetoes.

other choristers of the surrounding Forest will make known their joy, in their respective lays, at the re-opening of the portals of the Chateau of Mont Po. Martha, my beautiful horse, will be overjoyed at my approach, and expect the morsel of sugar which I invariably give to her, when I visit her: My faithful [Laclon], the most beautiful of the canine race, a Newfoundland, will display his accomplishments and manifest his affection to a manner peculiarly his own, in intelligence far beyond the level of the brute creation. Little Busy, a Scotch Terrier, with an eye as soft and expressive as that of a Gazelle, will be almost stark-mad with delight. He is the watchman of the house by night, and has his bed in my study during day. Apropos—a little dog in the inside of a house is more effective in terrifying robbers than a dozen larger one on the out-side. A Scotch burglar who had been convicted of his theft, and who had several times broken into the mansion of Sir Walter Scott, requested to see the illustrious romancer, before he was removed from prison to the penitentiary, in order that he might communicate some valuable information. An interview ensued. "Sir Walter," said he, "I never found any difficulty in getting hold of your plate. Reliable as you thought your locks were I could pick them as quickly as I could turn a key. A Scotch Terrier in the interior will alarm the house at the dead hour of night if he hears a sound at a door or window as loud as that of a pin-fall; and you may be sure that the most audacious robber will be so frightened, lest he may be caught, that he will be but too glad if he can safely retreat form the premises." Tam O'Shanter, the Solon of cats, (which I have carefully instructed from his early kittenhood,) is already on the qui vive for me.[81] He has passed the winter with me and is more improved by his social intercourse with the gay world than many a Yankee would be in double that time. He is thoroughly well bred and well-mannered. His robe is fur, as long and snow white as the finest ermine. He is of the purest Angora species, as playful as a lamb and quite as innocent. In his general deportment he is more like an affectionate dog than a resentful cat. This is not strange considering that Busy has been his constant companion. I could relate many thinks [sic] concerning

---

81 Tam O'Shanter was the subject of Mann's novella *The Life of Tammie Chattie*, which he published in 1872 under the pseudonym Tuckahoe.

his wonderful performances for the amusement of Anna, but I have already encroached too much upon your patience, when my Letter can be better employed.

4 O'clock. I have just come in form a long ramble through the most attractive and active portions of the City. The day is one, the like of which in all that is soft, and bright, and thoroughly genial to life, is scarcely experienced in a twelve month. The thousands of shops, from the largest to the smallest, are arrayed in the richest attire. They, alone, who constitute an Exhibition for the admiration of the most fastidious tastes. All the winter fashions have disappeared and spring is as handsomely represented by handicraft, as she will be a month hence in the gardens, and fields, and forests. Never any where before, was there so rich a display of luxurious articles for the consumption of use of women, and children, and men. I passed the last hour in the Garden of the Tuileries, my favorite resort at 3. The scene presented to the sight was more like that of a vision of a Fairly Land than a palpable reality. It was one from which "the Gods" could not have turned away with indifference. As I contemplated the innocent little children from ten ears down to infancy, assembled in thousands in the most becoming apparel, I could not help exclaiming "Yes! Of a truth such in <u>purity</u> must be "the Kingdom of Heaven." I could hear in my mind's ear, more distinctly, than I ever imagined before, the gentle voice of our saviour kindly rebuking his Disciples,"Suffer them to come unto me and forbid them not." What a blissful world were this if Angelic childhood could be carried through life to the grave of old age!

The Exhibition will be, certainly, opened on Monday. The note of busy preparation, to that end, is heard in all directions. That day will render Paris the <u>recognized</u> "Metropolis of Civilization." The hour, too, is rapidly hastening when she will be fairly entitled to the designation of the <u>Capital</u> of the world, for she attracts the barbarians from afar, as well the Turks and the Persians, as the Chinese and Japanese. All knelt at the shrine of her multifarious enchantments and [sources] of rational pleasure. May there not be in this an indication that the sublimity of our Redeemer's Mission is to be ultimately acknowledged all over the earth? I confess to you that I think so. "In hoc signo vinces"[82] encourages the belief.

Among the Confederates now here is the charming family of Gen. Preston of S.C.[83] I was at an elegant entertainment at their residence the other night, where I remained until 4 in the morning. Doct. and Mrs. Darby are great favorites of mine.[84] Gen. and Mrs. Breckinridge are devoted friends of mine, and will soon go to Mont Po to stay with me for a time. Gen. Toombs,[85] I perceive has arrived in Augusta! Truly "wonders will never cease"!!! When we separated he assured me that he was merely going to Havana to meet his son-in-law and would speedily return; and he said much more which I dare not mention in a Letter.

May our Heavenly Father prosper and protect you in the severe trials to which you are subjected. Give my love to your darling.

Believe me, Dear Mrs. Keitt, devotedly your friend,

---

82 A Latin phrase meaning "In this sign you will conquer." The sign was a monogram symbolizing Christ.

83 After the war General John Smith Preston (1809-1881) of South Carolina traveled in Europe until 1868.

84 This was Dr. John Thomson Darby (1836-1879) and his wife Mary Cantey Preston Darby (1840-1891). She was the daughter of Gen. John Smith Preston.

85 Robert Toombs (1810-1885) of Georgia was the first Confederate Secretary of State and later a general in the Confederate Army.

Ambrose Dudley Mann, Boulevard de la Madeleine, Paris, to Mrs. Sue Sparks Keitt, Charleston, S.C., c/o Mowry & Co.[86]

14 May 1867

My Ever Dear Friend:

In my last I informed you that I was about to quit here for Mont Po. Accordingly I arrived there on the 7th of April. Just as I reached the summit, upon which our mansion stands, (about noon), the sun, which had been obscured during the morning by thick clouds, appeared in all his splendor, brightening and warming the earth until he sunk beneath the horizon. Never did early spring present a sublimer spectacle of elegant nature. The scene to me was as lovely as Hope and as endearing as the most benign Reality. I fancied that I gazed upon the very Rose which beautified life's enjoyments, but how deceptive are all subluminary pleasures. Beneath the Rose there was the Serpent concealed, which was to strike me down. In less than twenty-four hours I was prostrate upon my bed, from an attack of Spasmodic Asthma, from which I expected never to be able to rise again. After three day's [*sic*] of intense suffering I was sufficiently relieved to make my way back to Paris, where I have had the best of medical attendance and where I have, at length, regained my accustomed health. Thus admonished it would be to trifle with my life were I to ever return to that little Paradise, in all else but my own heath, which I had created in my mind two year ago. Hostile as it is to me, you cannot imagine my good friend, with what reluctance, indeed with what anguish of heart, I forsake it. The incident is typical of all on earth to which we cling most dearly. I had looked forward, with thrills of delight, to the time when I should be favored at that charming retreat with your society and that of darling Anna. How much you would have enjoyed it! It is not the fault of the property that I cannot abide there. Unhappily it is the fault of my poor undermined constitution. The pure air is too penetrating for my susceptible lungs, which though sound have ever been weak. The Spasmodic Asthma, unlike the ordinary Asthma, is not chronic. It

---

86 Mowry & Company were factors and commission merchants in Charleston. One of the partners, W. S. Mowry, resided in Bennettsville, S.C.

is superinduced by atmospheric influences, and yields to the same agencies. It disappears in the impure miasma which engenders Cholera, and the various types of fever!

I have located myself in the very center of the heart of Paris, within a stone's throw of the Madeleine, in a delightful apartment, un premier. I intend to devote myself to literary pursuits. My fondness for reading has become a passion, and I have material enough to write out, to fill many volumes.

Be assured, my good friend, that I will not fail dear little Anna. I accept with unbounded pride her guardianship, and shall make it my study how I can best serve her should she be left motherless during my life. I shall even think of her as if she were my own sweet child; and never cease in my prayers to invoke the blessing of our [Righteous] Father upon her head. I am waiting to improve a little more before I have my Photograph taken I have a large sized one, very well taken, which I design for Anna, when I find a safe conveyance for it. In the mean-time do not forget to see me your own and General Keitt's.

My physician is Sir Joseph Olliffe.[87] He is eminent as a gentlemen as he is a professionally, and is close by. For the last week he has permitted me to go out between 12 and 3 every day, as that I can in the midst of the moving world. What a distraction from home and its attendant and surrounding cares and sorrows if you were even here with me! In my promenades! How long is this pleasure to be denied me? Sad, sad are the pictures, even to the sickening of the heart, which you draw of the South. Is it treason to the "Union" to say that our people are worse than Polandized?[88] You may dare not say so, but I who am not a victim to the rule at Washington can say so, and do say so as Heaven is my judge. I am sure the South has made a grievous mistake in accepting instead of acquiescing "in

---

87 Sir Joseph Francis Olliffe (1808-1869), a native of Ireland, was educated in Paris and practiced medicine there, and was honored by the French and British governments for his work.

88 This references the partitioning and destruction of the Polish-Lithuanian Commonwealth in the previous century. One of the U.S. Reconstruction acts partitioned the South into five military districts and established martial law therein.

the situation." Acceptance alienates admirers—<u>acquiescence</u> would have won friends all over the world. The South has made itself a party to the Martial Law Rule. This subject is so painful to me that I will dismiss it; and to move readily because I know it afflicts almost to madness your pure heart.

Pray write to me often. I cannot express to you the amount of comfort which your Letters afford me. They are as dew to the flower.

This is the first time that I have written since my attack, and it has been something of an effort to [race] over so much paper. Excuse imperfections. In future direct

"Monsieur Dudley-Mann.

17 Boulevard de la Madeleine

Paris, France"

Kiss little Anna for me and believe me always your devoted and affectionate friend,

Ambrose Dudley Mann.

[P.S.] Put your Letters into your Post-Office, marking on the corner "for British Steamer." It is necessary to pre-pay to ensure their coming. On one, the weight of this twenty cents, I believe, is the postage.

Ambrose Dudley Mann, 17 Boulevard de la Madeleine, Paris, to Mrs. Sue Sparks Keitt

23 June 1867

My Ever Dear Mrs. Keitt:

Bishop Lynch brought to me, three days ago, your esteemed Letter with its precious accompaniment.[89]

How much I thank you! It is so <u>like</u> <u>him</u> at the time we <u>parted</u>—alas! to meet no more on earth. There it stands conspicuously upon my mantelpiece, admired by all who enter my parlor. Gen. Preston and Gen. Breckinridge came in shortly after I placed it there, and gazed upon it with moistened eyes. But I may not say more this connection lest I open afresh the wounds from which your heart has already bled as much as mortal can bear.

You confirm my worst fears for the future of the South. I cannot find so much as a grain of comfort, as concerns the bettering of her condition, in any intelligence which I receive. Her ruin, politically, is already complete, while socially her degradation seems to be inevitable. All the ruling power of the North appears to be resolutely and actively at work to make the negro her merciless master.[90] Nothing short of a miracle can arrest the mighty arm that is uplifted against her. Of the ultimate breaking up of the "Union" or rather the <u>ci-devant</u>, <u>soi-disant</u>[91] Union, into many fragments, I have not the shadow of a doubt; but it is not likely to occur sufficiently soon to enable our people to counterpoise the strength which the demons our Congress have imparted to the black population. To behold public

---

89 Patrick Neeson Lynch (1817-1882) was the Catholic Bishop of the Diocese of Charleston, S.C. During the last year of the war he was in Europe as a Confederate commissioner seeking papal recognition of the Confederacy. In June 1867 he traveled abroad again to attend ceremonies commemorating the death of St. Peter in Rome.

90 In 1867, the first Reconstruction Act authorized military officials in the South to register voters, including freedmen. Other federal legislation forbade the vote to any person who had been an official of or aided the Confederacy—this while "six Northern States refused any Negro the right to vote, referendums in four were reaffirming this refusal, and the District of Columbia was refusing it by 7,369 to 36." Wallace, *South Carolina*, 571.

91 Former, so-called.

wrong, without the power of alleviating it, is an almost distracting spectacle to the philanthropic statesman, where his contemporaries are its victims. It is like looking upon the conflagration of a building wherein are woman and children who cannot escape and who cannot be helped. I often think that I would have more peace of mind if I were away off in some secluded spot in the Ionian Isles.

I am sure that Anna under your instruction is advancing rapidly enough. Let me urge you again not to confine her too much to the house. Of all earthly blessings there is nothing to compare to good health; and its seeds must take deep root in the earliest years of existence. I almost relinquish the hope of ever seeing either of you. My constitution broke down with the break-down of my poor country. Until then I was young <u>under</u> my years—now I am old <u>beyond</u> them. My good Physician tells me I must drop my pen forever, but I disobey him as relates to yourself. He says that while my Lungs are perfectly sound my Chest is too weak to bend over a desk. Thus I shall be deprived of one of my chief enjoyments. An amanuensis will be very awkward to me.

The Parisian world is going along gloriously, splendidly, joyously. It is estimated that there are well nigh a million of foreigners here at present. The Pasha of Egypt has arrived, and the Sultan is to come next week in great State. It is rumored that we are also to have the Sheik of Persia. His Celestial Majesty, it is said, has expressed a desire to see "the <u>doings</u> of the outside world and the Exposition." Hundreds of his subjects are in attendance, apparently chock full of joy. The Emperor and Empress of Austria, the King of Italy, the Queen of Spain, and the King and Queen of Portugal will arrive about the 1st of July. The two great Northern Potentates, after a stay of two weeks each returned to their respective Capitals. Queen Victoria will probably come at a late period, when she can be more en <u>famille</u> at the Tuileries.

I rejoice that you have such a delightful little locale for your own place of abode. Mr. Middleton, I presume, is a relation of Mr. Henry Middleton, whom I so well knew here 15 or 20 years ago.[92] Pray

---

92 "Mr. Middleton" was Williams Middleton (1809-1883), a signer of the South

take good care of your eyes. So not write more than you can help. I suppose you will go to your Plantation Home[93] for the summer and autumn.

Remember me most affectionately to darling little Anna. I long to see her and to greet you both in this <u>san souci</u> land.

Ever your Devoted Friend,

    Ambrose Dudley Mann

Carolina Ordinance of Secession. He owned the beautiful plantation near Charleston known as Middleton Place, and a fine house at 1 Meeting Street in Charleston. Williams Middleton was the son of Henry Middleton (1770-1846), and had a brother named Henry Middleton (1797-1876).

[93] "Plantation Home" probably refers to Mandeville in Marlboro County, S.C., her father's plantation.

Ambrose Dudley Mann, 17 Boulevard de la Madeleine, Paris, to Mrs. Sue Sparks Keitt, Charleston, S.C., c/o Williams Middleton

10 February 1868

My Ever Dear Mrs. Keitt:

My long and deep concern, for yourself and your darling, was relieved by your affectionate Letter of the 8th ultimo. I feared that one or the other of you was suffering from severe affliction. My imaginings sometimes went even beyond a sick bed. I thank God, with all my heart, that Anna has been restored, and I pray that you may both hereafter enjoy uninterrupted health. I, myself, have enjoyed the best of Heaven's boons since I last wrote. In fact I am now as strong and active as when I was in life's meridian. But my mind is ever and anon sadly [diseased] at the prostrate condition of our once happy land, and all the more when I reflect that such noble spirits as you are compelled to bear the iron yoke of a despotism that would have disgraced the hardest hearted monarch that ever reigned. In your rare powers of description you bring this vividly to my view. I see it alas! alas! too distinctly for my peace of mind. Think not, my good friend, that I shall ever break with my cherished purpose not to behold more the sunny South. I would rather go ten miles further from it than one mile towards its utterly blighted future. If I could have yourself and Anna with me, I should be less free from anxiety than I shall continue to be while you are subjected to so many risks and privations. Can you not tear yourself away from your torments? Do, I beg you, make the effort. Place her under my care, so that her salutary advancement may be assured, and you can make occasional visits to your old Plantations, in the interest of your affairs. You know I cannot claim my <u>guardianship</u> as long as you live. Were she an orphan I would <u>demand</u> her at once. The Photograph which you enclosed is different from that which I previously received, and I think much better. She must be very handsome, and her expression indicates a large promise of brilliant mind.

I am now beginning to look so much like myself that I shall venture to have a Photograph taken expressly for you; and I shall probably enclose it in my next. In the meantime be so obliging as to have one prepared for yourself, for transmission to me, if consistent with your inclination. I shall prize it most highly as you know—giving it the first place in my collection as well as in my heart.

There are still many Southerners here, less in most instances, in devotion to our cause than in name. There are very few who do not socially amalgamate with the abominable Yankees. I have no intercourse with any but the <u>truly faithful</u>, and of course my circle is but small. I have many esteemed acquaintances, however, among Europeans, But I go out but little. I am almost constantly occupied with my <u>work</u> which I expect to make the <u>chef d'oeuvre</u> of my life. It will be contained in three volumes in "<u>sketches</u>" and will not appear while I live. I write for posterity, and in the interests of truthful history. This week I shall complete the first volume. Pray write wherever you conveniently can do so Your Letters are invaluable to me.

                Ambrose Dudley Mann

[P.S.] Paris is less gay than usual this season. It over exerted itself during the Exposition. Still it is the most charming city in the world. How much you would enjoy its easy life! My devoted love to Anna. Guard carefully her health. Let her have good air always. Be not afraid that she will be too tall. She will probably not exceed your own height, which is a perfect standard for females. Withhold candy and sweetmeats from her as much as possible. In their too free use is the germ of dyspepsia.

Ambrose Dudley Mann, 17 Boulevard de la Madeleine, Paris, to Mrs. Sue Sparks Keitt, Charleston, S.C., c/o Williams Middleton

20 May 1868

My Ever Good Friend:

Your last, with its precious enclosure, was duly received.

Happily I had not heard of the attack of Anna until I was informed of her recovery. Pray take the best care of her. Let her have an abundance of open air exercise, but at the same time guard her carefully against the scorching rays of the sun. You are all in all to <u>each other</u>; but there is at least one far away heart that would be extremely saddened if either of you were afflicted by severe disease. Oh! how I wish you were both in this delightful climate, incomparably the best, the year round, in the world. How thankful I am for your beautiful Picture. It carries me back, so vividly, to the days of joy and hope when I first met you at Washington. What a future of bliss, as far as [human] eye could penetrate, seemed then to be in ready attendance upon your footsteps through life! Alas! the deceitfulness of the most reasonable earthly expectations. Such is my own melancholy experience. I was once so happy that my content was absolute. It would have been arrogant presumption in me to have wished for more. But while my heart was thus overflowing the Avenger suddenly came. Like yourself, I was left with a solitary child.[94] In him, and in memories of the departed, I <u>lived</u>. In all else I merely <u>existed</u>. For the first years I sought exclusiveness of my [race] and cherished grief, yes, <u>cherished</u> it for its very <u>sake</u>. I found myself rapidly drifting into incurable misanthropy. To extricate myself form its tyrannizing embraces I repaired to distant lands; beheld strange faces, strange customs, strange scenery. Soon the whole face of nature became changed to my vision. A ministering hallowed voice softly whispered in my ear "<u>become cheerful</u> and you <u>will be rational</u>. Become useful to your kind and you will be good in esteem of our Redeemer." Then I took up the thread of life where it

---

[94] Mann's wife, Hebe L. Carter Mann, died in 1849. His only child was a son, William Grayson Mann (1833-1896).

had been snapped, resolving never more to despair. So, I am now a Philosopher, feeling all afflictions "as a man," but "bearing them like a man." To nurture grief is to war with reason.

If you could get away from the sphere of your cares, that which has occurred to myself would most likely also occur to you. I most ardently desire and a consummation; and speedily, on your own as well as Anna's account. Her dawning intellect should not be impressively embraced with sorrowful remembrances.

Johnson, we are informed by the Cable, is acquitted.[95] Good may come of it. The "Infernals" will probably break with one another, and "Negro Suffrage" fail in the division. This is the only ray of hope I see for the South. As far as I can judge the Northern States will carry themselves against Negro Equality within their own limits. In that case they will resist it in the Southern States. This will be the issue in the Presidential Election.[96] Hence I begin to take an interest in the result.

I expected, with this, to convey to you my Photograph; but it is not yet ready—such as one, at least, as I wish so true a friend as yourself to possess. In my heart it will certainly go. Of my Book I have not space left to detail its [plan]; but will do so hereafter. I may remark that it is designed for posterity, not to be published until I am gone. I trust that you have good prospects for a Cotton crop, as well as other field productions. You deserve an abundant yield for your energy and industry, apart from everything else. With devoted love to Anna, your description of whom so delights me. I pray you to believe me, my excellent friend, Yours Devotedly,

Ambrose Dudley Mann

---

[95] Eleven articles of impeachment were brought against President Andrew Johnson by the U.S. House of Representatives in March 1868. On May 16, the Senate voted not to convict Johnson on one of the articles of impeachment, and soon afterwards failed to convict him on others. When Johnson left office the in 1869, he "issued a public statement accusing the 'servants of the people' [Congress] of betraying their trust, of exposing 'to the poisonous breath of party passion the terrible wounds of a four years' war,' and of legislating for special interests so that 'the few might be enriched at the expense of the many.'" Johnson, *North Against South*, 238-39.

[96] Ulysses S. Grant (Republican) and Horatio Seymour (Democrat) ran in the 1868 U.S. presidential election.

Ambrose Dudley Mann, 17 Boulevard de la Madeleine, Paris, to Mrs. Sue Sparks Keitt, Society Hill, S.C.

27 August 1868

My Ever Dear Friend:

Your charming Letter, dated July 15, but Post-marked, "Charleston August 11," arrived this morning. Seldom in my life, have I had such an enjoyment as its pleasure afforded me. Certainly none so sweet for many, many years.

Your sketch of the condition of political affairs in America, expressed my own views upon the subject as clearly as if it had emanated from my brain. I have but little more confidence in the integrity of Northern Democrats than I have in the integrity of the Radicals.[97] Neither the one or the other have any regard for <u>principle</u> when <u>interest</u> can be benefited. This fact was fully established in the inauguration and prosecution of hostilities against the South. The Democrats, in their greed for grain, were as eager for the fiendish war as the Radicals. They were not animated, in the slightest degree, by a sense of right, from the commencement to the end of the struggle; and now they are actuated by no other motive than the debasing one of lust for Power and its attendant profitable Patronage. I detest them all alike. Of Patriotism they know nothing and of public virtue they will learn nothing. They will employ the most unscrupulous political means to attain the end of material prosperity. I am proud that they are no longer countrymen of mine. As a cosmopolitan I am freed from such an inglorious association. Never let it cross your mind, my beloved friend, that I will identify myself with them again. The noble spirits of another world, who fell in support of the noblest cause for which sword was ever unsheathed, forbid it; fidelity to the memory of the founders of the "Old Constitution" forbids it; more than all my self-respect forbids it. For the world's wealth I would not seem to be that which "I am not;" and I cannot, nor ever can be, loyal to such a government as the Federal government. I hate its Flag as I hate no other Flag that ever was unfurled. I consider it, in fact,

---
97 Radical Republicans.

as a <u>floating</u> disgrace, in view of the deliberate crimes committed under it; as a <u>positive</u> disgrace to enlightened civilization. If I shall stand alone in my devotion to our overpowered cause be confident that I will <u>so</u> stand, as long as I stand upon the earth. I shall see my native land no more, unless, indeed, as I dare not hope, I shall see it <u>Independent</u>. The severest deprivation, in this regard, is to be denied the pleasure, I may say the bliss, of enjoying your society. I have many attachments in the South, but none that weigh a feather in the scale when contrasted with that which bonds me to yourself and darling Anna.

In the Presidential contest I take no interest, beyond an ardent wish to see a result that will precipitate the North into a long and sanguine civil war. I wish to see our merciless destroyers tormenting one another with as much ferocity as they tormented us. It distressed me to see some of our distinguished Generals co-operating so <u>zealously</u> in the Convention in New-York.[98] To <u>kiss</u> the hand that was <u>clenched in smiting</u> is the lowest degree of abjectness.

I most cordially approve of your system of instruction for Anna. It cannot fail to be as salutary in its influence as it is original. Such lessons she can never forget. Books as auxiliaries to learning are invaluable, but the most useful education is obtained out-side of them In your method you impress yourself upon your willing pupil, and no impression on her juvenile mind can ever equal that, in real worth. You gradually open the doors to extended knowledge, and in after years she will explore every field where there is a likelihood of a continued augmentation. You familiarize here with the whole world, and subsequently Books anxiously perused, and travel, will eventuate in an enlarged understanding of it. I, like yourself, love to indulge in fanciful contemplations of the mysterious beautiful. There is still more in nature to comprehend, for the benefit of mankind, than has never yet been comprehended. What a sublime study! The morning twilight—[unbedimmed] Aurora!—with Venus up in an hour or two in the Heavens apparently struggling to maintain her brilliant twinkles! What a spectacle! and yet how few of earth on account of the selfishness of easy slumber, ever behold it! As I sit

---

98 The Democratic National Convention was held in New York City in July 1868.

at my window and meditate upon this Celestial splendor, I feel as though I were prepared to enter the portals of the Great Invisible. I realize the Patriarch's vision of the Golden ladder let down from Heaven, and Angels descending and ascending, with glad tidings.

My circle of acquaintances is very large, and I am thus drawn more into society than I wish; but I never depart from the regularity of my habits. I make no more visits than I can with propriety avoid, and have no intercourse, whatever, with Northerners.

My "sketches," employ two hours of my time every day, except Sunday. Lord [Lytler] says this is as long a period as an Author ought ever to devote, in 24 hours, to his desk.[99] I am progressing finely. I design my work to be embraced in three large volumes. It will run over a period, if my life shall be spread, of sixty years, commencing with my first recollections of public men and public events, the war of 1812, when I was seven years old. The first will close with my departure for Europe in 1842. The second with my departure from Washington for Montgomery in 1861, and the third with the termination of my earthly career. Without being aware of it I find I have adopted the idea of Tallyrand, who provided, in his Will, that his Reminiscences should not appear until 30 years after his death.[100] That period has now elapsed, and was so announced the other day, and his work will be the book of the age, in view of the curiosity to peruse it. How much I should be benefited if I could have you near me, as I proceed to criticize my manuscripts! If you can arrange to come you will need no other protector for yourself and Anna than myself. When you fatigue of Paris I will travel with you where you wish. I am quite alone. My son and his wife are off in Switzerland. They intend to live to themselves. I advise this course. Mont Po I visit occasionally, but cannot stay there long, on account of the too thin and penetrating air. My health at this time is excellent. I take my morning walk upon the Terrace around the Tuilleries, which is free to promenaders during the absence of the Imperial family.

---

99 This possibly refers to Lord Bulwer-Lytton (1803-1873), an English politician and a prolific author.

100 Charles Maurice de Tallyrand-Perigord (1754-1838) was a French diplomat and clergyman. His memoirs were not published until 1891.

Then I occasionally, after I finish writing, take an airing in the Bois.[101] There is not a walk or a drive on the face of the globe comparable to the one and the other. Oh! My excellent friend, how much my happiness would be increased if you were here with Anna to join me in both! Why could not your [fancied] visit to me, and the agreeable surprise, have been a reality instead of a fiction? If it is within the possibility <u>do make it such</u>. Jefferson Davis and his family are still in England, where they are delighted. I expect them here. Gen. Joe Johnson has arrived.[102] The Slidell's[103] are at the sea-side. The Perkins, with Miss Izzard of S.C., are at Spa.[104] The Breckinridge's [sic] are at [Niagra], as also the Mason's[105] and [Proctor's]. I am "Amnestied." For what? Echo answers What? I despise the act as much as I abhor the actors. It places me however, out of the danger of <u>robbers</u> <u>alias</u> Confiscators. Pray, good Mrs. Keitt, favor me with your delightful letters as frequently as your convenience will allow; and with many kisses of my heart for dear little Anna, believe me

Your devoted and ever affectionate friend:

Ambrose Dudley Mann

---

101 The Bois de Boulogne, a large public park in Paris.

102 Joseph E. Johnston (1807-1891), a notable Confederate general, had commanded armies in both the eastern and western theaters of the war. After the war he found employment in a London-based insurance company, and sailed for Europe in 1868 to visit its home office. Apparently he also visited Paris.

103 John Slidell (1793-1871), a native of New York, and a U.S. Senator representing the state of Louisiana, was appointed as a Confederate diplomat to France. After the war, he and his family resided in Paris.

104 This refers to John Perkins (1819-1885), his wife Evelyn Harrison May Bayly Perkins (1819-1897), and his step-daughter Evelyn Mary Bayly (1851-1929). Perkins was a former Confederate Congressman and official, and a close friend of Jefferson Davis. Mrs. Perkins was the widow of Thomas H. Bayly (1810-1856), a Virginia Congressman.

105 James Murray Mason (1798-1871) of Virginia was a Confederate envoy to Britain and France.

Ambrose Dudley Mann, 17 Boulevard de la Madeleine, Paris, to Mrs. Sue Sparks Keitt, Charleston, S.C., c/o Williams Middleton

28 September 1868

My Ever Excellent Friend:

At least Levitsky,[106] the renowned Photographist of Europe, assures me that he has been perfectly successful. I enclose a specimen copy which he handed to me this morning. He says he can produce nothing better. Still, I fear that it will not realize Anna's expectations. She may find it so austere and severe in expression as to imagine that there is but little kindness in my disposition. If so I must trust to your bringing her over soon that I may convince her to the contrary. You probably, from a distant recollection of me, will not be much disappointed. Time and Care have left their ineffaceable marks upon me, and yet I have reason to be thankful that I am not more changed in my appearance and or my constitution.

Two weeks ago I wrote a long letter to you in reply to your last estimable one. Therewith I transmitted a Photograph of the Imperial family of France;[107] of which I presume you have been in receipt for some time; and I expect to so learn in due course.

I more grieved than ever that circumstances over which you have no control, fasten you down in the South. The aspect of affairs there as I behold it at this distance increases in darkness. Every arrival from New York brings more and more distressful intelligence. South-Carolina, or rather what once was South-Carolina, seems to be particularly doomed to annihilation as concerns all that Constitutes a State. With a prepondatory influence in numbers, the negroes, and their instigators, will never, I apprehend allow the respectable whites a moments peace of mind. In a war between the

---

106 Sergei Lvovich Levitsky (1819-1898) of Russia was one of Europe's most well-known photographers. His son Rafail Levitsky (1847-1940) was also a photographer and an artist.

107 This was the family of Charles-Louis Napoleon Bonaparte (1808-1873), who ruled France between 1848 and 1870, first as president, later as the last French monarch (Emperor Napoleon III).

races, the odds if Grant shall be chosen, and chosen he inevitably will be, the odds are all against you. The indications furnished by Vermont and Maine are broad enough for me to comprehend that a change has indeed been progressing in the North but in the sense of "from bad to worse." The "Infernals" are more numerous and more revengeful than ever. Grant has no fitness for his post, or rather his country's post, except his pliancy as a tool in their bloodthirsty interests. There is no longer, unless by a miracle the shadow of a chance for his defeat.

How grateful I am to the Almighty that the iron yoke of the soi-disant Federal government is not upon my neck. How sorrowful I am that one so much beloved by me as yourself should be subjected to its galling weight. I would gladly hope for your deliverance from its torments, but alas! I cannot while you continue to abide in the sphere of its operations. And darling Anna too. What a joyless future contrasted with that bright one to which she seemed to be born! May it be avoided by your extrication from a worse than barbarian rule! Existence without Life is the severest of all cruelties to which humanity is submitted and there is nothing beyond mere existence, for the elevated of character in the South. I pray you then, as soon as you possible can to come and take me by that agreeable "surprize" [sic]. What a day of bliss your arrival would be!

How are your cooks? Are the negroes respectful to you–I mean those in your service? Industrious I am sure they are not.[108]

Gov. Orr seems to have lost his prominence.[109] Gen. Hampton is certainly conspicuous enough.[110] I wish he had kept away from the

---

108 After the war, the freedmen who had once worked her father's plantation as slaves became "industrious" tenant farmers at Mandeville. "With few exceptions, [Mrs. Keitt's] relations with her tenants were harmonious." Merchant, *South Carolina Fire-Eater*, 196.

109 James L. Orr (1822-1873), a native South Carolinian, was governor of South Carolina from 1865 to 1868. He had formerly served in the Confederate States Senate.

110 General Wade Hampton (1818-1902) was a South Carolina planter and politician. During the war he became Lt. Gen., commanded Hampton Legion, and he was elected governor of South Carolina in 1876.

Convention, for his own sake. He is too noble a spirit to have mingled "With the White Spirits and Black The Brown Spirits and Gray"[111] of a concern which is animated by no higher motive than the attainment of place and power. I wish it success only in order that it may have courage and strength to [inaugurate] a Northern Civil War. I have no more love for Seymour than I have for Grant.

Ex-president Davis is still in England. He has placed his children at school in Liverpool. I am unadvised as to the time that he will visit France.

Mont Po has yielded finely this year. In quality I have never tasted finer fruits and vegetables. My table is supplied exclusively from there. I go out occasionally. My excellent physician assures me that ere long I can return there for a permanent residence if I choose. My health is now perfect. This to me, when most of the world is still away is, par excellence, the charming season of Paris.

Morning Twilight! Have you enjoyed the spectacle? The other morning Venus and the waning Moon came out together and did not separate until Aurora utterly dimmed their lustre. It was a sight for the Gods, and I can but believe that Ministering Angels invited me to behold it. I fancy I have [course] with them at such an hour, by far the most interesting one to me in the 24.

In writing to yourself, small as is my hand, my sheet is never large enough. Would you believe that this has been written without the aid of spectacles? I have never employed them in writing. My son and his wife returned yesterday. They talk of going in two weeks with her father and mother to Savannah. The father is well nigh 75 and [finds] it necessary to look after his affairs. The daughter is an only child, about 20. The father is unwilling to go without the mother, and the mother is unwilling to go without the daughter and the daughter will not go without the husband, Hence there

---

[111] This may be a reference to the 1866 National Union Convention in Philadelphia, which was attended by James L. Orr. It was organized to rally political support for President Andrew Johnson. The *Evansville Journal* of Indiana called it the "Butternut and Rebel Convention" (butternut brown and gray).

is no alternative for myself but to submit to his expedition. With many kisses to dear Anna believe me My Dear Mrs. Keitt, always your devotedly attached friend.

                Ambrose Dudley Mann

P.S. I have been in a painful quandary. I <u>have</u> a Photograph, but I cannot get my consent to enclose it. It is not sufficiently perfect. It is too austere—too rigid and too frigid in expression. It would shock Anna; and impress her unfavorably. This I must avoid, for I want her to love me; which I am sure she will do if I do not forestall her by a horrible out-line of my features. I will try again and see if I cannot get something better. I beg you to pardon me for the disappointment; for the continued non-fulfilment of my promise. I know you will do so. I trust I shall be soon enabled to comply. I send you the Imperial family, the most perfect I can find. In order to be in time for the nearest steamer I have dashed over my sheet with a sort of locomotive velocity. Pardon imperfections of style I beseech you.

Ambrose Dudley Mann, 17 Boulevard de la Madeleine, Paris, to Mrs. Sue Sparks Keitt, Charleston, S.C., c/o Williams Middleton

11 December 1868

My Very Dear Friend:

Your most kind & interesting letters, of the 15^t and 25^t November, have been received, the former on Sunday and the latter yesterday. I cannot suffer a mail to go off to New York without an expression of my profoundly grateful acknowledgments for their obliging contents. I enjoy no pleasure comparable to that of reading your correspondence and conversing with you in reply.

I am truly delighted that the Photograph is so acceptable to yourself and so much admired by dear Anna. All my acquaintances, who have seen it, pronounce it a wonderful success, even for Lavitzki, as natural as life and artistic to perfection. I now reproach myself, inasmuch as you so delicately reproach me, for not having complied with your request for it, long ago. How honored I am by your friendly esteem! as manifested in regard to this picture. How happy I am that Anna should prize it so highly!

At last I see a ray of hope of your coming. I shall fondly indulge the belief that it will, before the end of May, become a positive reality. It will be one of the most joyous days of my life when I shall welcome you both to the shores of my adopted land, "La Belle France."

You say you need "recreation, and rest, and petting." Where upon the earth's surface can you enjoy the two former in such perfection as here? And as to the latter I promise that you shall be the special object of my devoted attentions, even though I should incur the risk of the jealously of darling little Anna. You shall be exclusively <u>my pet</u>–the pet of all my affections.

My Dearest of Friends, a change of scene is essential to the restoration of your peace of mind. With all my composure of character I should soon go stark mad, were I subjected to such tortures as those inflicted upon you in your daily observations and experience. I am amazed that you support your trials and your cares with the patience that you do. Your soul is too noble to submit it to such wrongs. To live under Yankee rule is to endure an ignominious existence. "I would rather be a dog and bay at the Moon" [112] than a <u>willing</u> vessel of the government at Washington. Nor is there the shadow of a chance that matters will mend. As <u>a South the South</u> is politically crushed out of being. Oh! how I grieve for the true-hearts which have no alternative but to stay and bear the iron yoke imposed upon them by demons.

I am in expectation of a visit from ex-President Davis. He is still over in England, but writes to me from time to time, most affectionate Letters. I love him more than ever.[113] As in prosperity as in adversity, he is my devoted friend. I think he will locate himself permanently in Europe; and I trust so near me that we can be in constant intercourse. But he may have to go back to Richmond in March, to attend the mock trial that the Yankees are prosecuting against him.

I have never ceased to enquire for your female friend, but have not succeeded in ascertaining her whereabouts.

Paris has assumed its winter gaiety. It is again full. The shops are now all decking themselves out for Christmas, and the Churches will soon be dressed in verdant apparel. What sights for Anna, aye, even for yourself, as you have never been here at this season. I never fatigue of them, for they are always new and various. What a tasteful, inventive, people!

Now, My Dear Good Friend, let me implore you to dismiss your cares and anxieties, in your resolution to tear yourself away as soon as possible from a land which is causing you so much anguish. Your sensitive nature has been already too severely tested. Do not let it be harmed any longer. When you arrive we will put our heads together and see how much good we can accomplish for ourselves, and for

---

112 A quote from Shakespeare's *Julius Caesar:* "I had rather be a dog, and bay at the moon, / Than such a Roman."

113 Varina Davis wrote that Davis and Mann "loved like David and Jonathan, until extreme old age." Davis, *Jefferson Davis*, 1: 557.

others deserving our friendship. Write to me as often as I am inclined to write to you. No, that would be too much for you. But write once a week, as a diversion from sad thoughts; as a [salutary] medicine for a sick soul. Kiss Anna for me, and tell her to love me always. I send herewith an illustrated newspaper which may amuse her, and some slips that may interest yourself.

Believe me, My Dear Mrs. Keitt, Yours with devoted Affection

    Ambrose Dudley Mann

Ambrose Dudley Mann, 17 Boulevard de la Madeleine, Paris, to Mrs. Laurence M. Keitt, Charleston, S.C., c/o Williams Middleton

20 February 1869

My Ever Dear Friend:

Although I had written only a few days before the arrival of yours of the 25th of November, I did not suffer a steamer to depart without an acknowledgment of my obligations for that highly prized Letter.

Since then, now well nigh three months, I have had no tidings whatever of you. So long a silence causes me to fear that your health is not good or that my Letters failed to reach you. Pray relieve my anxiety as soon as you can, conveniently, after this is placed in your hands.

First of all, I am impatient to know whether or not I am to count upon your visit to me during the Spring. By this time you have perhaps decided. I need not reiterate with what joy I shall hail your coming, accompanied as you will be by my dear little Anna. Certainly there is no mortal on earth whose presence would afford me <u>so</u> much pleasure or whom I would endeavor to make <u>so</u> happy. "A Bohemian," though you say you are, I know your qualities, of heart and head, as thoroughly as if I had been in daily social intercourse with you every day, since our long and mournfully eventful separation.

If, however, you are forced by surrounding unyieldy [*sic*] circumstances, to remain in the land of iniquitous Yankee Rule, I shall utterly despair of beholding you more this side of the eternity.

You will have seen in the Newspapers that, after the Christmas Proclamation of Johnson,[114] I had determined to return. <u>You, I know</u>, did not believe the assertion. How could you after my numerous assurances that no earthly influence could produce such a departure from my purpose? Letters pour in upon me, urging me to re-unite myself with my noted country, but my eyes are closed to

---

[114] On Christmas Day in 1868, President Andrew Johnson issued an amnesty proclamation that pardoned all former Confederates.

all such entreaties. I have a heart which they cannot reach, because it is incapable of fraternizing with evil spirits. To accept the existing Union would be to become a part of it, and to voluntarily form a part of such a fiendish concern, with my convictions upon the subject, would be to dishonor me in my own esteem and thus dishonored, life would be hateful and happiness beyond the grave an impossibility. But observe the distinction between my case and the true hearts of the South–alas! alas! too few in number–who involuntarily submit. They have no alternative but to yield, for the reason that they cannot get away from their tormentors. Oh! that I had half the fortune that Rothschild left. I would be at no loss how to employ it. At once I would proceed to bring them–the truly faithful to the noble cause– to France and plant a Colony around Mont Po that would be in an ornament to Civilization. All their moderate wants should be cared for, and their children provided with the best of schools.

The South can never rise as a Power for the reason that she has been divested of the elements necessary for a successful independence. Then again she has, for the most part, been thoroughly Yankeeized in correct trickery and feasible hypocrisy. Villainy when it obtains a foot-hold or secures a habitation, is as infectious as malaria. In a word pitch will defile those by whom it is torched. If the Yankee [finds it] in his selfishness to his material, or other interest, to designate the negroes as "our respected colored fellow-citizens" his [surroundings] will readily, in the [west], from similar motives speedily adopt the same tender appellation. Downward tendencies are strangers to self-esteem and self abnegation. The elevated in sentiment are, and have ever been, too powerless to averrt flagrant wrong when cowering in triumph. Habit, for practical uses, is mightier than right. Hence political amalgamation of the two races can scarcely fail to be the initiator of amalgamation in its most revolting form. At this thought my heart sickens and for relief I turn away from the subject, horrified beyond endurance. But, I will add that the North, having accomplished its diabolical work, will crumble into atoms and will become the theatre of the [vilest] Anarchy that the world of mankind ever beheld–the inhabitants preying upon one another with an almost Cannibal ferocity. The late doings in Congress in the matter of the proposed amendment to the Constitution, foreshadows more perceptibly than ever, in any instance in human government before, that: "Whom the God's [sic] would destroy they first make mad."[115] If Heaven wills this then with all my heart I exclaim Heaven's Will Be Done.

I am just at the end of a sojourn, of more than six weeks, with one of my well beloved friend Ex-President Davis. He and Mrs. Davis came over on the 31st of December, she remaining for three weeks and then returning to her children in London. What a joyous time, what a breathing of sweetness from woe, what an incessant intellectual repast we had! During that active period we never broke bread asunder. My frugal fare gratified their frugal tastes; and they declined all invitations to share the hospitality of any one else; freely and frequently as it was profusely offered. Once alone, he and I dined with Mr. Slidell; and they imposed the condition upon me that I should have no guests at my own table. But my female circle were not to be shut out from Tea, and they came in vast numbers; as alas strangers, who were not known to either of us by name. They deported themselves not only admirably but with singular impressiveness. The President's bearing was as noble as to more than realize the highest expectations that had been formed of him. He was a magnificent representation of Majesty in adversity—a more sublime spectacle to every beholder than Majesty in prosperity. I never was so proud of him nor so proud of the cause of which he was the Executive Chief. As simple in his habits as a child, as meek in manner as a retiring maiden, as kind in intercourse as though it was his special mission to impart happiness to others, he excited the love of every body. The French were entirely captivated with him. The newspaper press was enthusiastic in his praise.

They both spoke in the kindest terms of you. More than a dozen times I took occasion to mention you, and how much I had enjoyed your brilliant correspondence. I even told them that I loved and cherished you more than any living lady because of your unwavering devotion to the principles for which we had battled, and for your unconquerable spirit in the interests of immutable justice. I could

---

115 The 15th Amendment, first proposed in December 1868.

write a volume in relation to all that the President did and said while he was with me, most of which I shall narrate to you ever if, happily, we shall meet again.

Just here, a Letter comes in from Mrs. Davis written yesterday at London in which she says: "Mr. Davis returned safely day before yesterday, just after night-fall, and is much improved by his stay with you. Your generous hospitality will always remain a most pleasant memory to us. Perhaps, many people desire to offer kindness; but no one knows so well as yourself how to confer it gracefully. My very Dear Friend it seems as a [gap] in our lives, since we cannot say when we can go to you again" etc. etc. I still hope to induce the President not to go to America. I fancy I have staggered him a little in his intention.

Paris is as charming as ever. The gay season was short this year but brilliant. We are now a week in Lent, which is less rigidly observed than formerly. There are several Carolina families here, among them the Ravenels and Roses. In numbers the South is largely represented.

What progress is Anna making in her studies? She will be nine years old in a couple of months, the beginning of the period for learning rapidly. Your tuition is the very best she could have. I presume her instruction is your chief pre-occupation as it is your constant delight. Is she healthful in all respects? Does she take abundant outdoor exercise? Give her all the love form me that you can express, and tell her to love me in return with all her heart.

You may justly conclude, perhaps, that I have not written to you <u>wisely</u>, but, as far at least, as length is concerned, you will not deny that I have written to you well. Pray never let any thing that I may say to you get into the papers by chance.

And now, My Dear Mrs. Keitt, I must bid you an affectionate adieu until I hear from you. May God ever bless you both.

Ambrose Dudley Mann

Ambrose Dudley Mann, 17 Boulevard de la Madeleine, Paris, to Mrs. Laurence M. Keitt, Society Hill, S.C.

2 March 1869

My Dear Mrs. Keitt:

Yours, post-marked "Society Hill" Feb. 12, came to me two days ago, relieving my mind from anxiety, for such is the interest which I take in the welfare of yourself and Anna that I am uneasy when there is a long space between your Letters.

How sorry I am that your Photograph did not come along as you intended. Send it, I pray you, if it is not already on its way, by the first steamer from New-York. I <u>am impatient to see you as you now are</u>. I always have you distinctly before me as you were when we parted. Then I have your picture of a later period to contemplate and to admire, but I await that, with intense solicitude, which I adore in anticipation, and shall love as I love none other in my collection.

Oh! yes, how unceasingly have I remembered the Egg-Nogg and the other [desserts] which you relate! How much I was interested in your <u>success</u> at the great Presidential Dinner! I was almost as proud of the impression which you made as was your husband. You were the bright, particular star of the evening. Because of my <u>avowal</u> of your being so decided a favorite of mine you provoked the displeasure of a very distinguished lady who was at the banquet. I cannot name her here, but she <u>fancied</u> that she had a <u>valid</u> <u>claim</u> to <u>all</u> my admiration.[116] I remember, too, when through your partiality for me, at the [large] dinner which you gave at the Ebbitt House,[117] to Senators and Representatives, that I had the honor of supporting you to the table and occupying the seat on your right. Again, I remember our drive to the Capitol and our promenade back. How elegant and

---

116 Mrs. Roger A. Pryor (Sara Agnes Rice Pryor) recorded in her memoir that Mann escorted her to a reception in Washington, D.C., while her husband, a Congressman, was busy with governmental matters, but her memoir does not mention any incident of displeasure with Mann or Mrs. Keitt. Pryor, *Reminiscences*, 47-49.

117 Ebbitt House was a boarding house in Washington, D.C.

stylish you were in all respects; the only lady that I really ever took pleasure in escorting on the avenue, with a <u>single</u> exception. In short there is "not a word, a look of thine my soul hath ever forgot."

You dispel the illusion which I had so fondly indulged of seeing you in Europe this spring. Distressful as is the thought, I must summon resolution to abandon the hope of the joyous meeting that I had anticipated as a meeting more desired by myself than any other in this world. What visions of delight I had pictured for myself from your springs of knowledge and your pure rich flowing genius. I believe I could have relieved you from woe and made your comparatively happy during your stay, <u>however</u> <u>long</u>. I must endeavor to find solace for my painful disappointment, in increased assiduity, in the work in which I am engaged and in which I find additional interest as it progresses.

Be certain, My Dear Mrs. Keitt, that you can never say <u>too much</u> to me of darling Anna. In all that concerns the development of her character and the completion of her accomplishments I am scarcely less indifferent that yourself. How could I be, particularly after distinguished confidence which you reposed in me in case of casualty to yourself? I am encouraged to believe that she will never require my Guardianship, but if, in the Dispensations of the Almighty, it shall occur otherwise, you have not counted too confidently upon my disposition to do all that is possible to make her an honor and an ornament, a light and a blessing, to her sex. Music and Dancing are the most graceful of accomplishments. Favor her success in both; but not to the prejudice of more solid acquirements. <u>School her thoroughly in your own strong common sense</u>. In Geography and History she can have no better instructress. In her own language she should be perfect. She will need no other but the French; the French, however, in Parisian excellence of pronunciation.

I said so much in my last, which was written just ten days ago, upon political affairs in America that I will but barely advert to the subject now. More and more am I thankful to my Heavenly Father that I am not a citizen of the United States, that I have forever severed such relationship with a country so ruled and so fallen. In reading an account of the proceedings of the House of Congress, upon the occasion of the counting of the votes for President and Vice-President, my joy was unspeakable that I shared none of the dishonor of that dishonorable and dishonored government. Low as is the abyss into which it has fallen, downward, and still downward, must be its movement until it sinks into the deepest recess of the bottomless pit.

What perfect [harmony] in sentiment, what striking [coincides] of views, between ourselves—as you will see by my last— in relation to the course our Ex-President should pursue. By remaining away, like the Statue of Brutus, his "absence will be more observed than the presence of the others." I presume that no living man more enjoys his confidence than myself, and I am using every persuasion in my power to induce him not to return. But I stand alone in my purpose. The strongest appeals, and by his old friends and associates, urge him to the contrary. His aged brother, an octogenarian, too, desires to see him once more. Thus I have fearful odds to contend against. But I never despair when there is not a positive consummation. I shall send him, when I write, in a day or two, the newspaper article, and what you say for himself and Mrs. Davis. They will both be gratified with your kind mindfulness of them. I had a most beautiful Letter from him two or three days ago. He was last night at the great debate on the House of Commons on the Irish Church Question. He has taken an apartment for a short time.

We shall have the inaugural of Grant, if he delivers one, on Friday. I take no other interest in its utterances than that I would take in the utterances of a successful robber chief who had murdered, and takes without remorse the living of surviving wives and children, and indicating what his next atrocities would be.[118] Good in it, for the interest of humanity, there can be none, for universal suffrage exclusive of race or color, I regard as <u>un fait accompli</u>.

---

118 Grant's second term was "staggered by one spectacular scandal after another. Some of them touched the intimate friends of the President ... The scandals extended far beyond Grant's circle, besmirching the reputations of diplomats, judges, the vice-president, and congressmen ... some of whom had accepted bribes from Credit Mobilier, a construction company connected with the Union Pacific Railroad." Johnson, *North Against South,* 263-64.

March has come in upon us most boisterously. Every body has been in-door for two days. This is a grievous punishment to the Parisian world. The season is advanced beyond all remembered precedent; but here may still be a "lingering winter for the lap of spring."

My old friend Mr. Lamartine died yesterday at 79.[119] How happy my hours with him in years gone by! His correspondence is one of the most valued of all my autograph Letters.

My son is in Savannah. In a political sense he is there with my sore displeasure, and if we ever meet again it must be on this side of the water. Much as I love him I shall never indulge my affection at the cost of my conscience. I told him so at the first. A higher than a filial duty led him away, the duty of a husband to a wife. They talk of coming back this summer, but I fear not, as her mother is in declining health while her father is so infirm as to stand upon the brink of the grave.

Now, My Beloved Friend, have I, in complying with your kind request <u>so promptly</u>, made you "happy?" If you think I am entitled in the slightest degree to your thanks, manifest yourself by bestowing upon Anna, for me, a sweet kiss and send me forthwith the coveted picture.

I will not apologize for the length of this, because I know you like to receive a long Letter, although you may not like to write one. I shall send you a [journal], now and then, if I see things likely to interest you. May God ever bless and protect yourself and Anna, is the constant prayer of yours, faithfully and affectionately,

                Ambrose Dudley Mann

---

[119] Alphonse de Lamartine (1790-1869) was a French poet, historian, and statesman.

Ambrose Dudley Mann, 17 Boulevard de la Madeleine, Paris, to Mrs. Laurence M. Keitt, Society Hill, S.C.

9 April 1869

My Dearest of Friends:

How much you have honored, obliged, and gratified me by your precious enclosed! It represents you as in perfect health. Your features are more full than those expressed in its predecessor. The change is not to your disadvantage. You seem to be even more beautiful than when I last saw you. I imagine you have more <u>embonpoint</u>; just a sufficiency to grace more strikingly your elegant dignity. Anna, too, is improved in appearance. She must, indeed, be very handsome.

You most kindly ask me to visit you. Ah! no. Alas! that pleasure is forever denied me. I have a <u>conscience</u> to obey as well as an <u>honor</u> to preserve. I should do violence to the one and disrespect to the other, if I were ever again to enter the embraces of <u>Yankeeized</u> and <u>Africanized</u> America. When I departed from the South, in March 1861, upon my Mission to Europe, I took a solemn, silent vow that, unless I returned with a recognized Independent Country, I would never return. That vow is as sacred to me as life, though every other Confederate should submit to Northern Tyranny, that Tyranny, with its attendant brutality, shall never victimize myself. I am descended paternally from a family of the "Kentish men" who were not conquered, when England was conquered. I revere their inflexibility and I love to emulate their patriotic virtues.

I would be willing to travel the world's length to be with your dear self, inseparable and forever, but were I to repair to you, even <u>temporarily</u> I would have to admit that I did so <u>by permission</u>, and to accept <u>permission</u> would, as I conceive, be to acknowledge dishonor. The case of yourself, and thousands alike situated, is entirely different. You had no alternative but to stay and bear all the afflictions of beastly merciless despots. I, on the contrary was not within the pale of their operations, and therefore I would voluntarily bow my neck to their iron yoke if I manifested my allegiance to them.

More still: the day that I left Washington to enter the service of the Confederate States, I practically, and to all intents and purposes, expatriated myself from the United States. Shall I [crouchingly] ask for a re-establishment of my Citizenship–where negroes, and worse than negroes, Yankees–would not ~~ever~~ only be my Peers in rights but my Masters in rule? I have interests, it is true, in the South, but let them perish in such an overpowering conflict. A regeneration of sentiment must occur in the so called Union, before I can contemplate even a visit to it, with composure.

With your Anna, My Adored Friend, endeavor to make the most of the necessity of your condition. You are all in all to each other. Her instruction will constitute a pleasure which will chase away, by degrees, sad thoughts.

Ex-President Davis strongly inclines to go back. My powers of persuasion, to influence him to remain in Europe, are exhausted. His oldest daughter is to come to my care, on Monday, to go for a year to a neighboring Convent.[120]

I sent you by the last steamer an illustrated journal. Did it arrive? It contained the fashions, for ladies. The amalgamation, socially, of Northerners and Southerners here is nearly complete. I am positively shocked at the cordial intercourse. Mrs. Perkins, her daughter and the Judge went last night to the notorious Burlinghame's Ball![121] My intercourse is narrowing down to French, and other foreigners. You have no idea of the wild, ostentatious, ridiculous extravagance in the entertainments of Americans, South and North! Every propriety of good sense and good taste is disregarded.

---

[120] Margaret ("Maggie") Howell Davis (1855-1909), the eldest daughter of Jefferson Davis, attended a convent school in Paris for a few months. Mann met her at a Paris train station and escorted her to the Convent of the Assumption in Auteuil, a Paris suburb.

[121] Anson Burlingame (1820-1870) of New York was an envoy and minister plenipotentiary heading a Chinese diplomatic mission to Europe and the United States. On April 8, 1869, he gave a ball at a hotel in Paris.

Kiss Anna for me, with affectionate lips, and believe me, as long as life lasts, Your devoted and admiring friend.

Ambrose Dudley Mann.

[P.S.] Pray did you find in your library "The Last Principle." I am hard on my work. I trust that your mother, even now, has been restored to good health.

Ambrose Dudley Mann, 17 Boulevard de la Madeleine, Paris, to Mrs. Laurence M. Keitt, Charleston, S.C., c/o Williams Middleton

20 July 1870

My Dearest and Best:

How good and amiable to bestow such favors upon me as those just arrived. I now <u>see</u> you as I once saw you, and, if possible, ever more beautiful and lovely. What a preservation in despite of your agonizing sorrows and cares! The artist has had a perfect subject. I tell you so in all [ardor]. I am charmed with his performance. He could not have had a better subject, and he has done it full justice. As I write I cast my eye upon your features and almost imagine that I am conversing with you.

Oh! how sweet in contrast with all other earthly objects.

Anna's too is very fine. She appears to great advantage in [doublet]. I can see that gracefulness is natural to her; and I almost begrudge you the happiness of such a daughter. I am to have her upon one condition; and that would be so sad as to deprive life of one of its dearest joys. If you were gone from earth I would be without an object to remain for, except on her account. But when you come here in winter you will bestow upon me a joint interest in her.

Unfortunately my Portrait was varnished before it was sent home, and therefore, cannot be photographed yet awhile; but I will hasten, as much as I can, the day for the transmission of a copy of it to you. The Painting well-nigh represents life itself. Eminent artists and connoisseurs say they never saw anything better upon canvas.

How much cause I have to be grateful to you, my most beloved, for your cordial and prompt compliance with <u>every</u> <u>request</u> that I ever made of you. Your last brings the joyous assurance that you intend to write to me once every two weeks, in accordance with my expressed desire. Thus you fill the cup of my obligations to you to overflowing. Now we shall be in regular conversation at short intervals. Write, and write first as you think, on every subject which you touch. Trust me, as you say you do, "implicitly." It is needless for me to reflect that you are as treasured in my heart that Heaven seems to have placed a seal upon it to keep it true and pure for yourself. There is good will in it for every body, except the Yankees, but love in it for you alone.

As you say nothing of the health of your mother I consider it certain that it is restored, or largely improved. I consequently count the more confidently upon your coming. France is in war with Prussia, but it will, in my opinion, be of but short duration; and if it should be continued through winter it will be no hindrance to your free and easy ingress to Paris.[122] In the contest all my sympathies are with France. The South had [maintained] triumphantly their independence but for the aid which the North received from Germany in troops, money etc. etc., as I shall clearly establish in my work. I believe in retribution in justice and I flatter myself that it is soon to be visited upon the Germans for the coldblooded wrong which they inflected upon the Confederate States.[123] Louis Napoleon did not do all that he might have done legitimately to benefit us during the struggle, but so refined is the civilization of France that only two swords of Frenchmen, those of the two sons of the Duke of Orleans,[124] were thrown into the scale of the Yankees. It is a thrilling time here and I am kept in a state of delightful excitement at the noble [marching] of the soldiers in their departure for the battle field. Both nations are thoroughly armed, and otherwise prepared, for an engagement, and even before this reaches you the greatest military duel that ever was fought may be announced to you by telegraph.

What would I not give to have you on my arm of evenings as the hundreds of thousands of uncovered heads march along my Boulevard chanting at the tops of their voices and with resolute

---

122 The Franco-Prussian War was fought between July 1870 and May 1871. As a result, Germany annexed Alsace-Lorraine, Germany formed an empire, and the French Third Republic was established.

123 In his letter of July 20, 1870, Mann states that the North received troops and money from Germany, without which they would not have won the war, and that he would "clearly establish" this assertion in his memoir.

124 Prince Philippe VII (1838-1894) served as an officer in the Union Army for about a year along with his brother, Prince Robert, Duke of Chartres (1840-1910).

yesterday [*sic*] the [soul stirring] <u>Marseillaise</u>. To adequately describe the patriotic demonstrations would require another sheet, but your imagination can supply the deficiency of my statement. There seems to be something Holy in the enthusiasm.

Implant a kiss I pray upon the cheek of sweet, promising Anna for me, and believe me My Dearest and Best, your profoundly attached admirer,

        Ambrose Dudley Mann

P.S. Always write by <u>Cunard</u> <u>Steamer</u>. They depart regularly from New-York every Wednesday. The French steamer will likely be withdrawn between Havre and New-York, as the German already have been. All intercourse by North with the U.S. will be through England. With the exception of Russia all Continental Europe leans toward the side of France. Great Britain will be rigidly, as far as she can, neutral with preponderance of sympathy for Germany.

Ambrose Dudley Mann,
"One of the Three Commissioners of the Confederate States of America to Europe,"
pictured in The Illustrated London News, 4 May, 1861. Editor's collection.

*Carte de visite photograph of A. Dudley Mann taken by the
Le Jeune studio in Paris, in or after 1872. It was owned by Mrs. Varina Davis.
Courtesy of the Virginia Museum of History and Culture.*

Susan Sparks Keitt,
a carte de visite by the noted Charleston photographer George S. Cook.
Courtesy of the South Caroliniana Library, University of South Carolina, Columbia, S.C.

*Ambrotype portrait of Susan Sparks Keitt.
From the collections of the South Carolina Historical Society.*

This carte de visite of Anna Keitt was taken by George S. Cook of Charleston. From the collections of the South Carolina Historical Society.

*Jefferson Davis in 1875.
Wikimedia Commons.*

Jefferson Davis and his wife Varina in Canada after his release from prison. This photograph was taken in Montreal in 1869. Wikimedia Commons.

Col. Laurence Massillon Keitt of the 20th South Carolina Infantry Regiment in 1864. Courtesy Library of Congress.

Ruins in Paris resulting from the bombardment. Wikimedia Commons.

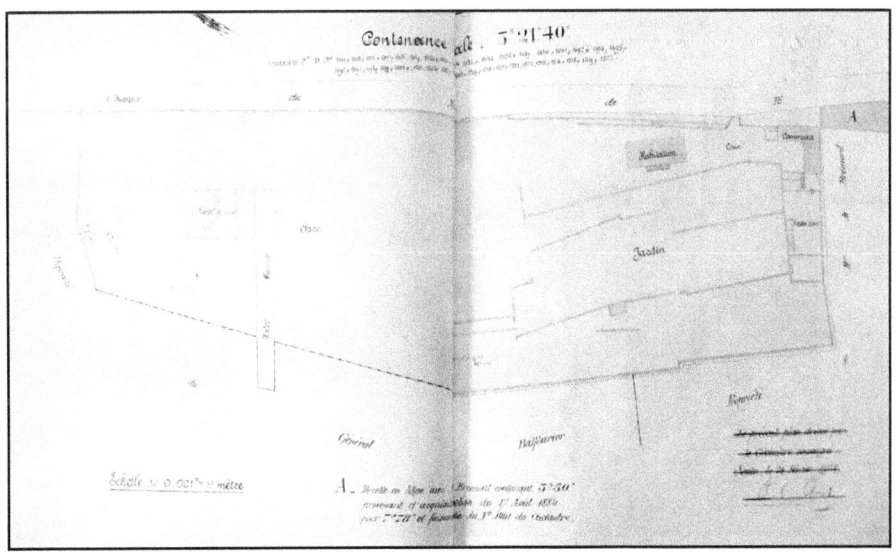

A land survey map of Mont de Po dated February 24, 1922, showing the habitation (dwelling), cour (court), communs (outbuildings), basse-cour (poultry yard), jardin (garden) et parc (park). Courtesy of Daniel Frankingnoul, CHAB.

*A bird's eye view of Paris in 1867 by Charles Fichot,
as seen from above the garden of the Tuileries. Wikimedia Commons.*

*The grave of A. Dudley Mann in Montparnasse Cemetery, Paris.
Hubert Leroy and other members of CHAB cleaned the gravestone and
affixed to it the Southern Cross of Honor. Courtesy of Hubert Leroy, CHAB.*

The burning of the Tuileries Palace in Paris by the Communards in May 1871. Wikimedia Commons.

This 1870 lithograph by Gaillard fils depicts the bombardment of Paris. Wikimedia Commons.

*A Communard barricade in Paris, 1871.
Published in Scribner's Magazine, 1887. Courtesy Library of Congress.*

Ambrose Dudley Mann, 17 Boulevard de la Madeleine, Paris, to Mrs. Laurence M. Keitt, Charleston, S.C., c/o Williams Middleton

4 August 1870

My Dear and Faithful Friend:

Two weeks ago I wrote to acknowledge the reception of the two splendidly beautiful pictures which you so graciously bestowed upon me. They are indeed charming – becoming from day to day so life-like that I often fancy that I am in the presence of the originals. If there were nothing else to concentrate my affections in you this much of devoted partiality for me would be sufficient to render my attachment ceaseless and ardent. It is the pride and glory of my life to be <u>so</u> <u>esteemed</u>; and in return I give you a <u>love</u> as <u>holy</u> as high, as <u>pure</u>, as <u>constant</u> as ever animated in human heart—not the love of mortal passion but the love of Celestial bliss. I ask no more of earth than that when I quit it I may live in your affections as I console myself that I now live. I know that, (as you say), you "implicitly" believe every statement which I make to you, and I should be false to my very notion if I uttered one which was not worthy of your belief. Therefore, make me your confidant in all things; that I may the more readily be useful to you in counsel. I must confess that I would be disturbed by jealousy if I thought you shared even in a slight degree, your confidence with others. You fill the place in my joys, here below, of my long departed one, who is in Heaven. Let me occupy a similar relation with yourself, during your separation from your lost one. Doubt not, fear not, they respectively, are in beatific happiness; basking in the never varying smiles of the Redeemer and intermingling with the just and good who surround them. In the immensity of space, so distinct to their visions, how puny must this terrestrial sphere seem to their uncircumscribed visions! While we are assured that there is "no marriage" "in Heaven" yet the happy marriages on earth are of Angelic [resemblance] with the <u>re-union</u>, in spotless purity of <u>spirit</u>, as is certain as that mortal <u>union</u> once existed [*sic*]. In our <u>soul's</u> eye we shall see and in our <u>soul's</u> heart enjoy. This, in my opinion, is the life Eternal and the Resurrection of the Dead—the spirits of the just protected by a constant association with the essence of Divinity. I know not if you agree in my views, but nevertheless I throw them out for your reflection, and if you do not concur in them I may be benefitted by your criticism.

This, I presume, will find you in retreat at your father's mineral spring, not to emerge therefrom until October. You can never be alone when darling Anna is with you. She constitutes your little world, which you can magnify at your pleasure. Contemplate her whenever you are sad; her present and the future which she promises to create, and new, joyous, hopes will loom up to dispel pensive thoughts. Endeavor always to "be of good cheer." Chase away every [obtruding-looking] care that has the temerity to carry itself against your peace of mind. Remember, with instruction, the delicate admonition to Martha. I am sure that you find much, in your surroundings calculated to weary and to worry you, but be ever your sweet self, and rise upon every occasion, superior to vexation.

I found myself, unexpectedly quick, at the end of my first sheet, and must commence a second in order to tell you something of the stirring events over here.

The Emperor is now at the head of his army, and such an army, so numerous, so disciplined, so enthusiastic, so supplied with all the accoutrements for sanguine conflict, the world never beheld before! In rank and file, with the resources, it must almost be at least 400,000 men, in the region of the Rhine. Germany has probably a still larger number facing it on the other side of the river. A battle is imminent between these enormous forces; and is not likely to be delayed beyond a few days. My judgment may be warped by my enthusiastic desire, but I am almost confident that the French will achieve a dazzlingly brilliant victory. You may have the intelligence by Telegraph before this reaches you. What a state of excitement we are constantly kept in! I in as much as the most patriotic Frenchmen. While I am not of a revengeful disposition I wish to see the life beaten out of that venal, servile people who furnished the "sinews" and the "brutes" to the Yankees, by which "my own, my native land" was conquered and subsequently humiliated. I would find in such a result a reasonable hope that Divine vengeance would not long be delayed in a manifestation against our degraded and remorseless oppressors. There is not in the Louvre a painting so replete with interest to myself as that which represents omnipotent justice, in its vengeance, pursuing crime. When I behold it I involuntarily ask, with closed lips: Oh Righteous Father, how long will this visitation upon Yankeedom be postponed? And I fancy that I am answered in soft accents: Trust in my wisdom, and in my unswerving Rule of Right and be patient. So I trust, and so trusting am perfectly confident.

Of dauntless heroism there can be nothing in this mighty war to suppress that which was displayed by our own armies; in self-sacrificing devotion to <u>cause</u> nothing to equal them. The Prussian, in hostile action, is a machine; the Frenchman a professional artist. I still think that hostilities will terminate with the first great victory of the French, and with a new political geography of Western Continental Europe. Neither side, on the face of its expenditures, can afford to go into winter quarters, preparatory to a spring campaign.

Now I have written as much as you will care to read this time, seeing that my correspondence is as frequent. Pray tell me is it as interesting to you as when you receive it at longer intervals? But why have I asked such a ridiculous question? Pardon me, I <u>know</u> my letters are always agreeable to you; because you so assure me. And by the same token permit me, My Dearest Heart, to remind you of your "<u>once</u> in <u>every</u> <u>two</u> <u>weeks</u>" engagement. Take the best of care of your health, and with the largest amount of love to Anna, believe me

Ever and Entirely Yours

    Ambrose Dudley Mann

Ambrose Dudley Mann, 17 Boulevard de la Madeleine, Paris, to Mrs. Laurence M. Keitt, Charleston, S.C., c/o Williams Middleton

19 August 1870

My Ever Dear True Heart:

Shortly after the departure of my last (Aug. 4), I was favored with the reception of yours of July 15.

What shall I say of its precious accompaniment? I have no words at command to adequately express my admiration. It is your sweet self, almost to the very life. I fancy that I can see the lips move and the timid blood gently flush your cheek. This is the language of a lover, and such I confess to be. If my so saying is unpleasant to you, you must blame nobody but Mrs. Sue Sparks Keitt, for her goodness inspires the avowal. This last mark of your favoritism, so delicate, so refined, and so graceful–draws you, if possible, still closer to the inner recesses of my heart. I imagine I cannot be mistaken, that you care more for me than for any gentleman living, or you could not be so faithfully mindful in contributing to my joys. In the indulgence of this hope there is but one more bliss that I could wish to enjoy on earth. That I dare not name, nor need I, for it will be of easy conjecture to yourself.

Much as I have been enchanted by its immediate predecessor I adore the present picture much more. It is in better taste as respects your apparel. Ample justice is done to your dazzling beauty. The expression is more natural. The features are better portrayed. The neck is more perfect: And the bust more elegantly arranged. The <u>tout ensemble</u> is a representation of modesty, and dove-like simplicity and purity of character. May I put it in a pretty little locket, and wear it–of course covered from human gaze? Now, pray do not evade this question my dearest, <u>ever</u> dearest one.

You ask if I will sanction your disrobing yourself of you dark apparel? I answer I wish it most anxiously. If you remember I implored you to so several years ago, as an effective means of securing a restoration of your cheerfulness. I would not have you forget the cherished object for which it is worn, but I would have you dispel unavailing regrets and overpower immoderate sorrow. You have, my beloved one, persisted too long in the indulgence of <u>gloomy thoughts</u>. A chronic melancholy is inevitable if you do not chase them definitively away. The affections of devoted wedlock are the noblest of humanity, but the Almighty never intended that, in the severance of that relation the one or the other, surviving, should be subjected to incurable anguish. In his restoration of his power to <u>afflict</u> he reserved also the power to <u>heal</u>. In this decree there is as much wisdom as mercy. While the lost one may never be regained still he may be replaced to such a degree as to create new hopes and new joys; and make life desirable. Such is the constant wish, I am quite certain, of those Celestial spirits of whom we have been bereaved. In our silent communion with them this is the counsel which they benignly bestow upon us. In early manhood, and for a period of ten years, I loved with an intensity and with a refinement which I cannot describe. For long years, though basking in women's smiles, in both hemispheres, and with many opportunities for contracting an alliance that would have gratified the highest worldly ambition of Diplomates [sic], Statesmen and Philosophers, I remained utterly unattracted and unattached. But at last a change came over me; and I find myself <u>loving</u> again with tenderness, the constancy, and purity, which ennobled my first affections. Can you reveal to me the mysteries of this strange fascination? Which has taken such active possession of me, and which for four years has made me so indifferent to all other women in the world beside. If I were in frequent visiting intercourse with you, perhaps your personal charms would afford the explanation. But as I have more than once assured you it is attributable in my opinion solely to heart and mind <u>sublimely acting on heart and mind</u>.

How ephemeral the bliss contained in your sweet consoling words: "Be happy; I will come."! Sadly as I am disappointed still more distressful as the <u>cause</u> which detains you. I condole with you in this fresh affliction and honor you all the more for your filial devotion. I trust, however, that your dear mother will yet recover and that her life will long be spared to you. How happy in having such a daughter constantly at her side. You will be to her, whatever the result, the Angel which I esteem you.

I am concerned for your own health, when you tell me you have "chills and fevers." They are undermining, usually, to the best constitutions, and you frighten me when you state that you are repressing them with Quinine. I never could be induced to taste that exacting medicine. Nor I never but once had it prescribed for me. It is too powerful for the strongest system. Try your best to do without it. Avoid all stimulants, even strong Coffee and Tea.

On your own account, and as a matter of pride, I would like when we meet to see you as I see you in your picture; but you would be none the less loved or none the less welcomed were I to salute you in snow white hair, wrinkled brow and furrowed cheeks. It is your glorious <u>soul</u> which I so much adore and with that I am in constant communion of Holy inspiration.

I shall be most happy to receive Monsieur de [Bellnigue]. If he had no other merit than that of being a "great friend" of yours, he would be entitled to my cordial regards.

[I] would go immediately to Carolina to console, aid, and pet you, in your trials and new griefs if I could do so without abridging my conscience. My honor, my duty, my inclination alike forbid my entrance into the confines of a Union which I so loathe, and from which I have forever separated myself. The South may rise again. I must reserve myself for the possibility. Strange political events are of constant occurrence. I <u>accept</u> nothing from the North and consent to nothing. Yankeedom is more alien to me than any portion of the habitable globe. Most of my living compatriots have yielded and are under its fiendish rule. <u>Necessity</u> is the plea. It is the plea also of the tyrant. The fallen in our battles and the women of your noble type alone reflect [lustre] upon our brutally overpowered wrong. I thank my God that in all things he has supported me with a <u>true</u> <u>spirit</u>, a spirit that will be equal to fidelity to the last. I am confident that you will <u>love</u> me for this though you may love for not other quality of heart or head. No, my Dearest, distracting as is the thought of our continued separation I cannot go to you except in a shame that would torture my self esteem. Hence if we never meet I am certain of your admiration to the end, indeed your devoted affection, as you are of mine. Try to be of good cheer always. Be your self and rise superior to every depressing influence. I read between the concluding lines of your too short Letter that a fit of melancholy had seized you, and that you had to throw down your pen, because of your tremulous hand. You know not how much this afflicts me. It will tell too, in after years upon darling Anna, if not corrected. This must not occur. Her life, which is opening so brilliantly, should be ever joyous. Oh! that my efforts had succeeded four years ago on drawing you to my humble country home, "Mont Po." That you would have had a charming stand point, form which wherever you chose we could have radiated not only to Paris, but all over Europe. Nevertheless, be resolute and hopeful of the future. If you were my own, as I in moments of forgetfulness fancy you are I could not write more freely or more enduringly. Upbraid me tenderly if I am too presuming; and attribute it to the intensity and constancy of my admiration for you. Ever as ever, Yours will all my heart,

                Ambrose Dudley Mann

P.S. So exclusively have my thoughts been engaged with yourself while writing my Letter that I find I have not said a word with respect to the war.

The joyous excitement which prevailed when I last wrote soon thereafter was succeeded by overpowering woe. The French, with three to one arrayed against them were beaten in the first battles. No body here was prepared for such a result, and hence the dismay. The tables seem now to be turned against the Prussians. We have cheering telegrams from the army this morning. My confidence in the success of the French Arms has never deserted me for a moment. The country is as united as if it constituted one man with a single will. The fighting thus far has sustained my belief that as a soldier the Frenchmen is vastly superior to the German. The odds in his favor is as two to three. The Crown Prince of Prussia[125] remarked,

---

125 The Crown Prince of Prussia was Frederick William (1831-1888), the son of

after his so called victory at Wissemburg,[126] that he would resign rather than meet his enemy with equal numbers. You, who have had such military observation and knowledge should look upon Paris as it is now fortified, for possible but not probable eventualities. The Yankees as I expected are warmly on the side of the Prussians. I hope that no true Southerner will have his feelings enlisted on the side of such cut throats. The <u>tri</u>-<u>color</u> floats gracefully in the breeze from my window. I can scarcely remain in my apartment, so great as my anxiety and profounding [sic] interest, longer than fifteen minutes at a time. Pardon this scrawl. I am called for on pressing business.

Take, I pray you, the best of care of your health. May God bless you and make you equal to your afflictions and the performance of your filial duties.

Do, write me a long, very long, Letter upon receipt of this.

     A.D.M.

---

the German Emperior Wilhem I (Kaiser Wilhelm). He would later become Emperor Frederick III.
126 The Battle of Wissembourg was the first in the Franco-Prussian War and resulted in a German victory.

Ambrose Dudley Mann, 17 Boulevard de la Madeleine, Paris, to Mrs. Laurence M. Keitt, Charleston, S.C., c/o Williams Middleton

1 September 1870

My Ever Dear Friend:

Your long silence, after your obliging engagement to correspond <u>fortnightly</u>, excites my anxiety for the preservation of your good health. I cannot repress my apprehensions that there is no improvement in the condition of your mother, and that, you are bowed down with grief and care. More, than ever before, I wish I were near you to assist, to solace, and to comfort you, in your fresh affliction. Was ever mortal subjected to a severer trial than myself, in my continued separation from you? The conflict between <u>conscientious duty</u> to <u>a</u> <u>cause</u>, which was dearer to me than life itself, and an affection, which is the predominating sentiment of my heart, is constant and arduous. To me earth has no joy equal to that which your charming society would afford; and yet I cannot release it, or rather am forbidden to so by the integrity which I have so devotedly cherished since, and indeed before, our overthrow. The relation in which I thus stand is like a tale of Oriental romance.

Tell me now <u>frankly</u>, my best beloved, my Darling Friend, would I not sink myself in your esteem were I to repair to you? I fancy that your partiality for me had its origin in your observance of my inflexible devotion to patriotic purpose; and that it has been increased by my unwavering fidelity to my principles. Were I, by any act of mine, to diminish your regard or your confidence I should sink under my self reproaches. If you were to conceive that my nature were less noble than you had believed it to be, there would necessarily be a diminution in your attachment to me, and you would regret that you had so confidingly, in case of an improbable but not impossible eventuality, bestowed to my tender guardianship dear little Anna, I have resisted the appeals of my excellent son and his excellent wife to go back to the South, as well as those of the President and Mrs. Davis, and indeed many other endeared friends. The thought has never yet entered into my mind to yield to their persuasions. The world would say, why hold out so obstinately in the presence of such examples and such influences? My answer is, that when I am summoned before the Throne of Thrones to give an account of my earthly pilgrimage, where I am to meet "the just made perfect," I wish to appear in self-assurance that I have never, knowingly, committed a violence against the "still small voice" implanted in my bosom by my Creator.

Again, I ask, tenderly and imploringly ask, what do you say? I take up your picture and accordingly survey its beautiful lineaments in the hope of interpreting your answer, but I fail. It must come from your own <u>thoughts</u> and over your own <u>signature</u>. But this may be obviated by a repetition of the enchanting promise–even though less positive as to time–"<u>Be happy</u>; <u>I will come</u>."

I trust, as I am in fact certain, that dear Anna is progressing to your entire satisfaction. If so her accomplishments, solid and adorning, will be equal to my utmost wishes. Fortify her constitution, during her months of relaxation from study, for vigorous application when they terminate.

And now of Paris, of France, and of the War. Since my last, written just two weeks ago, we have been threatened with a siege of 200,000 or 300,000 Prussians, for Prussians now mean Germans, or rather Germans means Prussians. I never believed in the consummation of such a project; but the Fortifications, the most stupendous on the earth's surface, have been prepared for such an eventuality, and all Foreigners modestly invited, by the authorities, to quit the Capital, while the [Prussian], and vagabond portion of the population, have been forced to do so. I resolved at the beginning that, whatever the woes of the French I would share them; and I have accordingly held myself in readiness to shoulder a Chassepot[127] for the defense of Paris. There is, to-day, not the shadow of a likelihood that it will be assailed. In that respect the public mind is now at ease. The notion was preposterous; at any rate in the absence of a decided victory of the Prussians in the region of Metz.

---

127 A bolt action military rifle used in the 1860s by the French army.

There has been no abatement in my confidence that the French in the end will be eminently victorious. They fight like lions, and the whole nation is aroused and eager for revenge. While they have had, in several instances, to retreat before vastly superior numbers they have [harmed] the Germans in the ratio of 3 to 2– in the aggregate whose losses in killed, wounded and missing are estimated at 200,000! Long before this reaches you the definitive battle will probably have been fought; and the intelligence thereof conveyed to you by the sub-marine telegraph. I [await] the event, as you may readily suppose, with thrilling interest and solicitude. In the success of the French I shall find streaks of light for the South and the eventual humiliation of cruel and arrogant Yankeedom.

I am expecting, or will expect shortly, President Davis. He is in London and is, with all his heart, on our side. The Radicals or Destructives are in co-operation, as far as they dare make demonstrations, with the Germans.

Miss Emily Mason is here, and is one of my daily visitors.[128] I told her how much you had enjoyed the perusal of her Letter, and of your kind expressions for herself. She was flattered by the recital. She, with her traveling companion, Miss Emily Harper, of Baltimore, go home in October. The Slidell's are at the sea-shore, near Havre. If a siege of Paris were possible it is amply provisioned for a twelve month or more; while the country is so barer for forty miles around– its products, of all kinds being stored here– that the besiegers, cut off from foreign supplies, could not subsist for a month. I never enjoyed "the gay metropolis" more than at present. There is as much life in it as in peace, and it is well-nigh exclusively French. Let me again implore you to write every two weeks. You must know with what thrilling delight I read the thoughts which you express. They are the joy of my existence. Your Faithful Admirer

Ambrose Dudley Mann

---

128 Emily Virginia Mason (1815-1909), a Virginian and a descendant of the Revolutionary War patriot George Mason, became the principal of a school for American girls in Paris in the early 1870s. Her friend was Emily Louisa Harper (1812-1892) of Maryland.

Ambrose Dudley Mann, 17 Boulevard de la Madeleine, Paris, to Mrs. Laurence M. Keitt, Charleston, S.C., c/o Williams Middleton

12 September 1870

My Dearest Heart:

(Yes <u>dearest</u>, for in the employment of this tender appellation I do no more than give adequate expression to my predominating affection) Why, Oh! why have you so long suspended your correspondence? I can imagine that the sick chamber of your good mother demands your undivided care and attention, but still there must be intervals in her affliction during which you can snatch a few minutes to write a short Letter.[129] I incline to the belief that you yourself are not well; and what a streak of joy would be that which would remove my anxiety in this regard! I have written to you, as I promised, once every fortnight, and your last was written at Charleston <u>two months</u> ago!

There is but a bare chance that this will reach you. The mail still leaves regularly, by a new route, for England, but there is no certainly that this communication will not be interrupted before to-morrow morning. The French are prepared to cut the railroads around Paris at the first signal of the near approach of the Prussians. While <u>I am slow to be convinced</u> that a Siege will be attempted almost every body considers that the event is inevitable. All our Southern friends, with two or three exceptions, have fled to other countries. From the first I resolved to stand my ground and share the fate of glorious Paris, so dear is my esteem. I abide in the very <u>heart</u> of its heart; and when the hour comes, <u>if</u> it do come [*sic*], for its defense, I shall shoulder my <u>Chassepot</u> and fight, to death, if necessary, against its inhuman invaders.

How have the great disappeared! "How have the mighty fallen!" since the date of my last to you. That gigantic name which was once the charm of France–I mean in the days of the first Napoleon–is now so prostrate that there is none so poor as do it reverence. In

---

129 Mrs. Keitt's mother, Ann Harry Sparks, died on November 13, 1870.

the hour of trial never did such incompetence manifest itself in a Ruler as in the Prussian prisoner Emperor.[130] The very name of Bonaparte is loathed and despised. Would you believe it, that, when the intelligence of the disaster to the French armies arrived, and the captivity of Louis Napoleon was confirmed, the towering column of Vendome, was stripped of its immortelles, in which those who until then worshipped it, or many of them, participated.[131] The next morning the whole Prussian world was out–a brighter September day I never beheld–and at three o'clock, or thereabout, the Republic was triumphantly proclaimed, without the slightest resistance or the spilling of a drop of blood. I was an eye witness of all that transpired.

General Trochu,[132] the head of the Provisional Government, is a noble soldier and inspires in the army, as well as in the population, not only confidence, but that which is more important for victory, energetic enthusiasm. Such a spectacle was never presented to mankind as the metropolis displays this day. It constitutes a military camp in which there are six hundred thousand able bodied men under arms! Then, there are in and on the Fortifications three thousand pieces of Artillery. Five hundred thousand Prussians are reported to be upon French soil. What a conflict, with such an array of antagonistic strength, must result, if a Peace be not negotiated in advance. I am as hopeful as ever of dear France; but what sacrifices in blood and treasure await here if the war continues! I will not imagine their immensity as I shall perhaps shrink from a computation of the realization. May it be infinitely less than I apprehend! France has not only her glory to re-establish but her shame to efface. No nobler motive could animate intelligent, high souled mortals.

---

130 The "Prussian prisoner" was Napoleon III, who was captured at the Battle of Sedan in early September 1870.

131 The Vendome column is a bronze column in the Place Vendome. It commemorates Napoleon's victory at Austerlitz in 1805. Immortelles are flowers that symbolized unfading remembrance and immortality.

132 Louis-Jules Trochu (1815-1896) served as President of the Government of National Defense, the first government of the French Third Republic, from September 1870 to January 1871.

We are amply provisioned for a two months' siege. If the water supply fails we can satiate or thirst on the delicate Claret, of which I chance to have a stock for two years. My good friend Mrs. Acosta formerly Miss Mary Carroll of the "Manor" of Maryland[133], has a supply of [Hautes][134] and she proposes that we shall share with one another to the last. Herself, her cousin Miss Carroll, and Mrs. Weston formerly of Virginia, are the only American female friends of mine now left. Since I took my seat an esteemed acquaintance from Baltimore came in, leading her son, an only child, of ten years of age to bid me farewell, while her husband was searching a conveyance to the rail-way station. They tore themselves away in tears, expecting no more to see me.

"He jests at scars who never felt a wound." I still bear the wounds of heart acutely, consequent upon our fall by brutal hands, and know how to appreciate the scenes of mortification to which the French have been submitted. I will stay and sooth their sorrows, and contribute to bind up any fresh wounds which they may receive. In this I know I shall have the approval of one noble heart at least–that which palpitates in your own bosom.

It may be weeks, possible months, before I write to you again. Continue, whatever your domestic cares, to make my darling Anna <u>the object</u>–the controlling object of your earthly devotion. Be always <u>yourself</u>, and you will be equal to any trial to which our Heavenly Father may subject you. I have your picture to console [me], whatever the emergency which I may encounter, and your partiality as evinced in your designation of me as Anna's protector and guardian, to encourage me should despair threaten.

A French friend, at this moment, runs in to tell me that a Telegraph has just been received, stating that the Prussian are within 15 miles of the outer Forts of the city and that a Proclamation is

---

133 Mary Carroll (1826-1902), the daughter of Charles Carroll (1801-1862), married Dr. Elisee Acosta of Paris. The "Manor" likely refers to Doughoregan Manor in Maryland.

134 This word, which is very difficult to interpret, may be "Hautes," perhaps referring to a wine or wines.

about to be issued that the gates are to be closed to-morrow, against all egress and ingress; and also, that rumors are current that the King of Prussia is disposed to treat for Peace.

Remember me, lovingly, to Anna, and believe me always, yours affectionately

   Ambrose Dudley Mann

Ambrose Dudley Mann, 17 Boulevard de la Madeleine, Paris, to Mrs. Laurence M. Keitt, Charleston, S.C., c/o Williams Middleton

23 February 1871

My Ever Dear Mrs. Keitt:

In a Letter which I received yesterday from my son I found enclosed your precious favors of Dec. 10 and January 18. Prior to their reception I was without any intelligence of later date from you than that contained in your short communication of July 16–written just as you were quitting Charleston. Therein you prepared me for the bereavement which has since afflicted you. My heart-felt condolences are with you in this as they have ever been in all your griefs.

I continued to write fortnightly to you until the Cordon Militaire[135] suspended mail intercourse with the outside. Then, from to time, I availed myself of the Balloon Post[136] sending you thereby a long printed document of my preparing which I imagined would interest you; but very often the mails thus carried fell into the enemy's possession or were destroyed in fear of such an occurrence.

A messenger connected with the [re-victualing] of Paris informed me a few minutes ago that he would convey this to London and start it for its destination. He departs in half an hour. Therefore I cannot now write as fully to you as I desire. When the surveillance of the Prussians over the mails terminate I will not be slow to gratify my wishes in this regard.

Need I assure you of my constant mindfulness of you, since during the trying ordeal through which I have passed. In thought, so faithfully do my affections cluster upon you, that you are always with one in the sense of a Ministering angel. How I regret that I did not five years ago hasten to your abode and throw myself at your

---

135 The encirclement of Paris by the Prussians during the siege of 1870-1871.

136 During the siege, mail was sent out by coal gas balloons. In November 1870, William Grayson Mann reported to Jefferson Davis that he had received several "several highly interesting balloon letters" from his father, one of which was meant for Davis. Davis, *Papers,* 513.

feet; imploring you to let me bear you away, with darling Anna, from the distressful scenes of your woes and cares. I think that you would have enjoyed Chantilly and its delightful society; where your father and mother could have joined us.

You tenderly ask: "Why did you subject yourself to such needless danger?" I reply, I was prompted alike by duty and inclination. I could not desert a people to whom I was so much attached in adversity's hour. My nature prompted me to remain with them to cheer and comfort them, and to divide their sorrows if sorrow came. Then, again, I was desirous of being an eye-witness, a minute observer, of the operations of the most wonderful conflict that has occurred in all time. Homer and Livy, as described by [men], were realised in the exciting interest. I would not, "for the sea's worth" have been away. Of suffering, I had none whatever; and my health was in perfection. In my life I never know any thing of the passion of fear; and danger, personal to myself, I did not in the slightest degree apprehend at any time. I hope one day or other to narrate to your ear, all the incidents of the eventful period. They will be carefully embraced in the concluding chapters of the volumes which I am preparing for posterity.

Cheer up My Ever Dearest. Be hopeful, confidently hopeful. Brighter days I am certain await you. I can never consent that you shall become an instructress, creditable as is such a pursuit. Let not your dismay reach that point of despair.

I think of quitting France in October, if I can wind up my affairs by that time. I cannot live amidst the misery produced by national humiliation. The spectacle is too sad for a soul as enthusiastic and a disposition as cheerful as mine. It is this sentiment that has prevented my return to my down-trodden country.

I rejoice to hear that my sweet Anna, is so good and so promising. Give her my kisses, and make known to her my devoted thoughtfulness in all that concerns her welfare. What a source of pleasure to me you and her Photographs have been! during the terrible crises.

In my next I will write more advisedly of my future plans. Answer this, I pray you, quickly and conceal from me nothing that relates to your well-being. My <u>address</u> is ever the same.

The messenger comes and I have to conclude abruptly and without time to run my eye over that which I have so hurriedly written, but not without an expression that I remain,

Yours with <u>all</u> <u>my</u> <u>heart</u>, as I would blissfully wish that you were mine.

Dudley Mann

[P.S.] In order that your Letters may with certainty arrive permit to suggest [*sic*] to you the necessity of writing upon the paper like this, and <u>pre-paying</u> sufficiently.

Ambrose Dudley Mann, 17 Boulevard de la Madeleine, Paris, to Mrs. Laurence M. Keitt, Charleston, S.C., c/o Williams Middleton

1 March 1871

My Most Beloved:

I wrote a hurried Letter to you a week ago, which I trust arrived in due course from London, where it was mailed.

I have been much distressed, that the thought of entering a Convent, with Anna, should ever have entered your mind. Your heart, and intellect, and person were not created for concealment from the world. They were intended for a high and useful sphere, such as for long years I have been so desirous to see you move in and adorn.

I pray you; My Ever Dearest, to utterly relinquish the torturing idea of placing your brilliant "light under a bushel." In the absence of a better title to your charms I claim them as my rightful companions; and I cannot, and will not, see them so [cruelly] sacrificed. I am sad, sad indeed, to be informed that you are weary of life, when you have so much to live for. I had indulged the belief, and was strengthened in it by me of your Letter last summer, that you had ceased to cherish your griefs and was [sic] gradually preparing to mingle again in society. It was natural that your recent bereavement should inflict new wounds, but not of such depth, considering the advanced age of the dear departed, as to be, for a lengthened period, incurable. In her instance nature was but acting out the rule of nature, from the beginning of the earth. Her sun, like that which ornaments a long June day, had moved steadily on until it sunk beneath the horizon, in conformity with the inflexible laws of the Almighty.

Of the political and pecuniary condition of dear Carolina, they are such as I from the first foresaw they would be; and implored you to escape from them. I see no chance, whatever, for an improvement. More than ever I look upon every thing American with horror. The governing, and also the governed, morale of the States is discreditable to civilization. I can find no [patience] to read a public document emanating from any source there. They are as hypocritical as they are base in concealed intention. Many of the former high-toned men of the South are succumbing, under their iniquitous influence, and are in close fellowship with negroes. Alas! alas! poor fallen people; to what extremities have they not already been driven, and to what greater extremities may they may not yet come. I am well nigh distracted when I contemplate the subject in all its bearings. Enough, enough of this.

Darling Anna! How I long to see her. I wish most ardently that she was with me. I should so like to instruct her myself in valuable knowledge rather than through books. Refined, varied, and intelligent conversation is the best education that ever was bestowed upon the young, of either sex. Convents and Boarding Schools fail in this. They teach too much that is <u>not</u> worth learning and too little that <u>is</u> worth learning.

You tell me of her flowing golden hair. Ask her to send me a lock of it, and if you will accompany it with one of your own you will additionally oblige me. If I <u>loved you</u> less I could not summon courage to make so bold a request. If I admired you devotedly before, I <u>adore</u> you now for your concern for me while I was in so precarious a position and for so long a time. Do not fail to send me the Letters which you had written and not forwarded.

The Prussians came in this morning and occupied the fairest portion of the metropolis, that of the <u>Champs Elysees</u>. By agreement they are confined to a district, running from the <u>Place de la Concorde</u> along the bank of the Seine two miles downward and extending backward to the <u>Faubourg St Honore</u>. The population is in tears at the humiliation. I cannot repress my own. I am within 100 yards of the Prussian lines, which are extended close to the front of the magnificent Church of the Madeleine, which you cannot fail to recollect as the most cherished structure in Europe.[137] Fears are entertained that in the agonizing exasperation of the citizens a collision may be precipitated, which will involve as all in [ruin],

---

137 The Eglise Sainte-Marie-Madeleine is an impressive classical building constructed during the reign of Napoleon Bonaparte, and was originally intended as a temple to celebrate his Grande Armee.

even to annihilation. The hour is momentous in the [extremest]; and still I was never more composed. Outside of the circle of occupation by the invader, the living City is as silent as the dead city of Pere la Chaise.[138] Such a morning I never witnessed. The telegraph will inform you of the <u>finale</u> long before this meets your eye.

Let me beseech you to arouse and shake off your cares. If I have to be thankful to Heaven for one thing more than another it is that it has ever blessed me with a cheerful, [confidently] and hopeful disposition. May it thus bless you is the prayer of yours. Most Affectionately,

        A. Dudley Mann

---

138 The Pere LaChaise is a large cemetery in Paris.

Ambrose Dudley Mann, 17 Boulevard de la Madeleine, Paris, to Mrs. Laurence M. Keitt, Charleston, S.C., c/o Williams Middleton

20 March 1871

My Ever Darling Friend:

I am favored with your short Letter of February 5. I am impatiently awaiting the arrival of another informing me of the reception of several of mine, written, one after the re-opening of mail communication with the outside world, so also those which you had previously prepared and kept back until they could certainly reach me. I do not wish to lose a word or thought of yours addressed to myself. They are as genial to my soul as the dews of Heaven to the flowers of June; in fact the joy of my life in my separation from the pure and true heart which prompts their utterance. Why, O! why, are you so penurious in their transmission? I will not attribute it to <u>indifference</u>; for I have abundant evidence to the contrary, of long years accumulation, amply corroborated by your abiding concern for me when you fancied that I was in danger from the effects of the <u>Cordon Militaire</u>. Considering our cordial sentimental relations, and the freedom with which I have expressed myself in my correspondence, from time to time, I sometimes think you are over reserved, if not positively fastidious, in your communications with me. Were I, however, ever sure that this was the case I could not find it in my nature to chide you, for that nature is incapable of chiding for anything one who has so large a possession of my affections as yourself. Accept, I pray you this avowed and this explanation, as delicately expressed as I know how.

You most kindly invite me to return to the land of my <u>hate</u> (as at present in humanly governed) upon a visit. In any thing else I would esteem a <u>request</u> of yours a <u>command</u>. While the South is endeared to me, by the fondest recollections and associations of my life, an eye-sight contemplation of it, in its sunken condition, would convert the smiles which I would gladly wear for friends into agonizing tears. Those used, from the first, to the manifold barbarian wrongs to which it has been subjected have become so accustomed to them that they can support their affliction with modest composure, but I, who have kept myself beyond the pale of their brutal operation, would deserve the torture, which would be inflicted upon, were I, even for a day to place myself voluntarily within their sphere. But in order to properly impress you with a sense of my almost idolatrous <u>love</u> for you I would forego my own discomforts, indeed the attendant wear and tear of conscience, if I could bear you off forever from the scenes of your sorrows and your cares. I have implored you, running over a space of five tedious years, to come to me. The fates have been against my invocations. I will continue in hope that my constancy of purpose will yet overcome them. If you will do all in your power to aid in my object the chances of success will be certain to multiply.

Suppose, My Ever Dearest One, that I should conform to your obliging request in what benefit, of increased happiness, would it be to either of us? The <u>meeting</u> would be sweet, at least to myself, but Oh! the <u>parting</u>! The one would be the Flower in all its fascinating innocence, the other the Serpent under it, of departing, despairing joy. Better, better far, that I should never enjoy the attractive charms of your society than sever myself from it with a <u>final</u> <u>Farewell</u>. I should be unequal to so heart-rending a trial. How transient, too, would be the duration of my stay! A summer's month at most.

Of France I am grievously, for the first time, fatigued; and I am already engaged in making my preparations to quit her for a more quiet land. I would not leave her in her deep distress if I saw any likelihood of her ceasing to <u>distress</u> <u>herself</u>. She is as incurably crushed by the Prussians as were the Confederate States by the Yankees. She retains a mere guest independence, nothing more. She is in a state of wild distraction, too delirious to know what to do or how to find relief. "How are the mighty fallen!" Her ruin is complete; the ruin of a solitary man – the worst of all the men that ever rose, or reigned, or fell, always excepting Lincoln, Johnson, Grant and their cohorts. In all times, from Cain down, a mightier monster has not appeared on earth, with this exclusion. Divine Vengeance, (in which I am an implicit believer) has been steadily in pursuit of him, until it has hunted him down, for his willful violation of his oath when he became President in 1848, and the French are now "in sackcloth and ashes" on account of their having dignified and legalised his [cherished] crime.¹³⁹ False swearing now, as in the days of old, is one of the most heinous offenses in the sight of the Almighty. A chief creed of my religion is, that <u>to war against truth is to war against God</u>. Apart from my own instincts upon the subject the blessed Redeemer emphatically so instructs me. In His last beautiful and affecting prayer, to His Father, in behalf of his disciples, he asks, Him to: "Sanctify them <u>through</u> thy Truth: <u>Thy</u> <u>Word is Truth</u>." A sinful world, may in its own belief, <u>dignify</u> a falsehood, but it is not given to humankind to <u>sanctify</u> one. As His <u>Word is Truth</u> so will He defend that <u>word</u> from His Throne of Thrones; until time shall be no more, against all the combinations and machinations of the wicked inhabitants of the earth.

But to return to the subject of my future abode I have decided to repair to Italy to bask in winter under the sunny skies of Rome and to retreat in summer to the balmy air of Milan and Como. There is quiet in that consecrated land of story and of song; and an abounding generosity of public and private sentiment. Rome, in the extraordinary vicissitudes through which Europe is passing, may become again that which Rome once was. She may arise from her long lethargy and assume her former high position as the Capital of civilization. Paris is likely to lose the enviable distinction; and where, in her disrobement, can her mantle fall but upon the Eternal City? I want to depart about the 1st of July and pass that month in my old familiar places of abode in Switzerland, and from thence proceed to the lake of Como to remain until the 1st of October. Then I will pass two months in Milan and go by Rail to Naples, and arrive in Rome early in December. This is an outline of present purpose, which is however easier traced than executed, for I have much to do in the way of winding up my affairs, before it can be accomplished. The Chantilly property, (Mont-Po) is yet to disposed of, as well as my nice little <u>ménage</u> to break up. There is pain in the thought of each; for I have a most comfortable home,

---

139 Charles-Louis Napoleon Bonaparte (later Napoleon III) was elected president of the French Second Republic in 1848. When he took office he swore an oath to "remain faithful to the Democratic Republic" and to "fulfill all the duties imposed upon me by the Constitution." Although it was unconstitutional, he succeeded (by a coup d'etat) in giving himself a second term, and in 1852 held a national plebiscite asking citizens if they approved of his new government. The questionable referendum was overwhelmingly in his favor.

surrounded by every convenience. If possible, I must go to England after the Easter recess of Parliament, to see my old and valued friends, before I leave Western Europe, to return no more.

Had you another daughter I would claim Anna and take her along with me to Italy, there to educate her, less in books than in conversation relating to what I have seen and heard, and approved and reprobated, in my large and long intercourse with human kind, accomplishing her in all that graces, and honors, and dignifies your sex. But she is all in all to you, and, therefore, her separation from you is not an idea to be entertained. Let her have the full benefit of your own salutary example and, I doubt not, she will be an ornament to the circle in which she is destined to move. I design, as soon as a private conveyance offers, to send her a testimonial of my affection for her; and to accompany it with a Letter.

You will learn, by the Telegraphic accounts, that Paris is, while I write, in a blaze of Civil War; and your interest in my security form violent harm, may cause you uneasiness. I do not know what will come of the present formidable belligerent demonstration of the perturbations, but I do know that I am not in the slightest degree concerned for my own personal safety.[140] The population which stood all the horrors of the Siege are flying by thousands, terrified as they were not terrified by the shells of the Prussians. The present emuete [141] is decidedly the most serious and the best organized that has occurred since the time of Robespierre, and yet I incline to believe that it will fail of its purpose.

Remember always to write to my usual address "Monsieur Ambrose Dudley Mann. Paris,. France, 17 Boulevard de la Madeleine." If I am not here your Letters will quickly follow to my abode. My love to dearest Anna.

Yours, with all my Heart,

            Ambrose Dudley Mann.

---

140 This was the Paris Commune, an insurrection in Paris against the government of Napoleon III's Second Empire.
141 Disturbance, or insurrection.

Monday March 20. Your <u>retained</u> Letters, dated, August 17 and December 10, came in immediately after I had concluded the preceding sheets.

They were more the less interesting because for their age; since they abounded in expressions of kindness and interest, More recent ones had apprized me of you loss, in reply to which I assured you of my heart-felt condolences. I now am awaiting fresh intelligence from you which I hope will be more cheerful than that conveyed in your last, informing me of your notion of going with dear Anna to a Convent, and becoming an Instructress therein. The thought of such an eventuality has distressed me more than I can describe to you. I am sure that the idea was but the fitful emanation of a moment of gloom.

Although I have never been without a decided opinion with respect to public men and public measures in Europe as well as American and have been not only unreserved but fearless in its utterance, yet where such utterance is painful to a friend whom I esteem I am careful in its suppression. I am too observant of the refined proprieties of social intercourse ever to cause a pang of anguish to those within my circle. As the admirer of Louis Napoleon, which you so exactly avow yourself to be, I beg you to skip over the sentences in my Letter which so severely animadvert upon him. I will only add, in this connection, that I am truly sorry of your want of knowledge of all his enormities. A <u>Republic</u>, such as was Virginia and South-Carolina in other days, and such as Switzerland is at present, is the best form of Government ever given to mankind. The "United States" never was a Republic. It was aggression, usurping powers that were not bestowed upon it, form the beginning of its existence, and this usurpation culminated in its becoming the most autocratic system that ever attempted to control the destinies of a people. As I have never ceased to adore the Sun, notwithstanding the black spots upon his beaming face, so shall I never cease to adore the self-governing system, as the noblest one, notwithstanding the crimes committed by those entrusted with its administration. These are my sentiments, My Good Friend, and if you cannot sympathyze [*sic*] with them be certain that I shall esteem you none the less. As I have lived so shall I die steadfast in my devotion to them.

But I will turn to a theme more agreeable to you as well as to myself. I am really honored by your candid reply to my current appeal for a more complete avowal of your confidence. I thought I was entitled to be the recipient of your <u>secrets</u>, in all that related to your personal welfare. I am delighted with your modest, [gracious] <u>confession</u>. I urged you, as delicately as I could, long years ago to break with your unavailing griefs and take up with life and its attendant pleasures again. Wisely have you, at last, conformed to my wishes, in accordance with your own inclination. Do you thoroughly know yourself when you state that you are inexorably resolved never to surrender your independence? never to marry? Time, with its varying concomitants, is such a mighty [arbitrator] upon human purpose, in the matter of the <u>tender passion</u>, that except in any rare instances that <u>purpose</u> is of a finally yielding nature under the stress of forcible circumstances. As concerns myself I would, indeed, if you could be equally happy, prefer that you should remain as you are, in your single state. But in this desire I must own there is <u>selfishness</u>. I am ambitious to continue, as I fancy I have been all along, <u>first</u> in your esteem as a <u>friend</u>. This would be precluded were you to consent to become the partner of the joys and sorrows of another. I would be alike deprived of your confidence, and of you correspondence except in polite formality. Thus I should be robbed of one of my most cherished pleasures. However dear to me such a consideration will not weigh a feather in the scale if you imagine, or rather confidently believe, that a <u>change</u> will be conducive to your earthly happiness. In such an event I need not pray you to be studiously careful in your choice. Be positively sure that the bliss which you will impart to the fortunate winner of your heart and head will be of reciprocal extent. You must bear in mind that you will be incomparably more <u>difficult</u> than before while your chosen one may be unequal to the <u>difficulty</u>. Nor must Anna be forgotten. Her bright future should be the permanent object of your life. She ought to be loved, though in a different sense, as devotedly by her step-father as yourself. I never saw the woman, with which, in his childhood's years, I would have placed my son in such an embarrassing relation. Where I chose to be I was invariably a favorite, and in the first circles of every land on which I sojourned, with the ladies; yet I involuntarily repelled every emotion of my heart which threatened the enlistment, in a matrimonial sense, of its affections. I rejoice that I did so; for he will revere my memory all the more because of my mindful affectionate constancy in his behalf. I have never been, in the slightest degree, in danger <u>Though not a man of the world in feeling. I am, nevertheless a thorough man of the world in general indifference</u>. The only exception is in your instance, as I have more than once assured you. I long ago became, fascinated with your character of heart and mind, entirely irrespective of your beauty of person; and I have nourished this fascination as a sublimity of the alluring <u>ideal</u>. Is not my love for you unnatural, unearthly? I shrink at the thought of meeting you face to face; lest, I may be as much overpowered by your presence as I am enchanted by your absence in the perusal of your communications. In conclusion if you carry out the line of travel which you have traced you may count upon my services in <u>every sense</u> that will be most agreeable to you.

How strange that I can write to you so composedly when Paris is in a state of the wildest commotion, the insurgents triumphant, carrying everything before them. I was in their midst all the afternoon of yesterday. While they were forbidding others they suffered me to penetrate the spots which they occupy, receiving me courteously. They were as kind and good natured as mortals well could be, and seemed to mean no harm. I was not in a higher state of excitement during the siege, and the awful shelling, than I am now. I start out now upon "my afternoon circuit to see more of them. So Farewell <u>until</u> I receive from you a recognition of this <u>long Epistle</u>.

A.D.M.

Ambrose Dudley Mann, 17 Boulevard de la Madeleine, Paris, to Mrs. Laurence M. Keitt, Charleston, S.C., c/o Williams Middleton

2 May 1871

My Ever Dear Friend:

There is again a suspension of mail intercourse with the outer world. It has already been of a month's duration and may continue much longer. I have, therefore, no Letters from you, a much [watched] want. A chance has just presented itself for a safe conveyance of communications to London and I avail of it to write a few lines to you, to express my unabated interest in the welfare of yourself and dear Anna. Did you receive my long, very long Letter of March 20? What are your present plans? What of your pair of admirers? Do they still woo without hope? Which is the favorite? Come now, "honor bright."

We are here in the midst of the most awful crisis that ever afflicted a nation.[142] The horrors of an intestine war stare me incessantly in the face. In death-like resolution the two armies war in full array against each other, battling incessantly day and night. Neither seems to win a decided advantage. Had they fought as well against the Germans as they fight against each other victory would have been certain and speedy. The supreme moment is, however, not distant. Paris may be in ruins in a week. I am in the very center of the contested district, the heart of the heart of the metropolis. How disgraceful such a conflict to civilization! I look on with [composure]. Afflicting as is the spectacle I would on no account avoid it, as it will perhaps constitute the most wonderful epoch in the world's history. What a generation is this in crime and other wickedness! There has been none like it in the calendar of civilization. It was [invigorated] by the perfidy of Yankeedom in its repression of the South. Retrogradation is the offspring of that false philanthropy which assumed the name of Progress. I detest the very word. Political knaves have kept it "to the ear" expressly for the purpose of breaking "it to the hope!"[143]

---

142 The Paris Commune continued until May 28, 1871.
143 Mann is quoting from a phrase in Shakespeare's *Macbeth* (Act 5, Scene 8),

But enough. Time passes. Pray let me hear from you. You made a good start to write <u>freely</u> and <u>fully</u>, as I requested. Do not withdraw your confidence or I shall really think you "<u>are in danger</u>."

Much love to Anna and believe me,

Ever Yours Affectionately

A.D.M.

---

referring to deceivers: "That keep the word of promise to our ear, / And break it to our hope."

Ambrose Dudley Mann, 17 Boulevard de la Madeleine, Paris, to Mrs. Laurence M. Keitt, Charleston, S.C., c/o Williams Middleton

1 June 1871

My Ever Beloved Friend:

In the first delivery of letters, yesterday, after a suspension of mail intercourse of nearly two months, I was favored with yours dated March 14, Post-marked New-York April 29! wherein you state, that, you had received nothing from me of later date than my hurried Note, carried out by Balloon in November. This information is as amazing as it is perplexing. <u>Immediately</u> after the Prussian Siege was raised, in February, I wrote to you, and repeatedly thereafter, in recognition, as well of your fresh as your old Letters, until communication with the outside world was stopped by the Mob-Commune at the end of March. Early in May I managed to get a Letter out to you, and enclosed another to my son. Of all my correspondents you were the first in my thoughts, and I accordingly wrote more frequent to you and at greater length than to any other. I was uniformly careful in directing to Mr. Middleton, and I cannot conceive how my Letters miscarried. I am thus explicit upon the subject, because I with you always to believe that I am utterly incapable of unmindfulness to one who commands so much, and so constantly my cherished affections as your always dear, good self. One of my Letters, of vast length, (running over no less than three closely written sheets, double to size, of this) I was most anxious that you should receive, and, I trust, that it reached you after you wrote, and that I shall be so informed by the next entrance of Letters, from Versailles. Therein I expressed myself freely and fully in relation to French affairs as well as of matters personal to yourself and also in indication of my own plans.

I am sure that it will interest you to know that I have passed through the recent <u>firing</u> and <u>fiery</u> ordeal unscathed and untouched, my health all the while as perfect as mortal ever was blessed with. Thanks to <u>Him</u> to whom alone thanks is due for such protection and blessing. My location was the safest from the out-side shells but the most exposed in the inside conflict. My "hair breadth escapes" were numerous but I was as indifferent to them as I was unconscious of them during the long fray. From the first to the last I was thrilled with exciting interest. The sensation of fear never animated me for a moment, and I was insensible to the danger which surrounded me. I ate as heartily and slept as soundly as usual, though enveloped in flames, in close proximity for thirty hours. The fierce fight, and the subsequent supreme victory, had its commencement on the other side of the Boulevard directly in front of my door. I calmly beheld it in joyous contemplation. With what reflective delight I gazed upon the triumph of <u>Order</u> over <u>Mobocracy</u>! But Oh! what a scene attended. Women screaming and bounding downward to the cellars for security, children crying, men palsied with fright! How my thoughts ever and ever adverted to yourself! How I wished you by my side, for <u>your</u> composure and courage of all the women of my acquaintance would have most harmonized with my own. You would have, perhaps, been aghast in wonder but not in apprehensions personal to yourself.

From the 2nd of April until the 28th of May, with the exception of a truce of ten hours to enable Neuilly[144] to evacuate and flee to Paris, there was, comparatively speaking, no intermission in the [sanguinary] engagements. Had there been half the vigor, endurance, and courage, displayed against the Prussians they would have been disastrously driven out of the country.

The Mob-Commune was the largest, best organized, and most desperate, body of robbers and assassins, that ever leagued together. It was composed of the evil spirits of every land.[145] The Yankees were not without fit representation in it. Its paramount object was pillage, at whatever sacrifice of life to the pillaged. It was by the merest chance they were not all burnt up.[146]

---

144 Neuilly, which is now known as Neuilly-sur-Seine, was a commune (municipality) near Paris. Part of Neuilly was annexed by the city of Paris in 1860.
145 "The Commune "admitted all foreigners to the honour of dying for an immortal cause." Marx, *The Civil War in France,* 23.
146 On May 25, 1871, *The Nation* editorialized of the Commune: "On the whole, the reign of the Commune ... strikingly illustrates the truth of the observation that the barbarians whose ravages the modern world has to dread, live not in forests, but in the heart of our large cities." Beckert, *The Monied Metropolis,* 180.

Order reigns to-day but the germ of revolution has already been planted again in the proceedings of the <u>Right</u>, in the National Assembly. The Thiers government it is believed, as meritorious as it is, will soon be upset.[147] A fusion of the two branches of the Bourbons seems to be inevitable and of [early] occurrence; and, perhaps, before you peruse these lines the telegraph will have informed you that <u>Henri Cinq</u>[148] the Legitimist, has been proclaimed King! I must own that I am indifferent to the result; although I intend to die, as I have lived, a <u>moderate</u> <u>Republican</u> such as was Washington, Jefferson, Calhoun and the glorious men of the South of their times. Come what may I will never be a renegade from my principles nor faithless to their memories. I am pressed for time, and therefore this scrawl. A post goes out this afternoon at four and I avail of it to satisfy you that my interest in Anna and yourself was never more [ardent]. All your cares I share, and have no regret <u>so</u> profound. as not to have it in my power to remove them. Try to be of good cheer, cease [inundating] yourself to your deprivations and the consequences. Of such alas! life is made up and humanity has no alternative but to accept the condition. I rejoice to learn that Anna grows in <u>beauty</u> under your judicious pupilage. I am sure that she is alike growing in useful knowledge. With constant love for you both

I am, as ever,

    Yours with all my heart

        A. Dudley Mann

---

147 Adolphe Thiers (1797-1877) was the first president of the French Third Republic.

148 Henri, Count de Chambord. He was a member of the House of Bourbon, the royal dynasty of France since the Medieval period. Although the restoration of a Bourbon monarch was seriously considered for a time, Henri never actually became king.

Ambrose Dudley Mann, 17 Boulevard de la Madeleine, Paris, to Madame L.M. Keitt, Bennettsville, Marlboro District, S.C.,

28 June 1871

My Ever Dear Mrs. Keitt,

Your two charming Letters, enclosed in the same envelope –one without date the other with that of June 2–arrived last Sunday.

How am I to thank you for all the tender expressions of affectionate interest which they conveyed? My heart was already bankrupt in devotional gratitude for your abiding partiality and constant mindfulness of me. Its offerings were equal to its resources, huge as were the proportions of those resources.

You <u>scold</u> so gracefully that I enjoy it more than I would the <u>praise</u> of any one else of your sex. I like it. In fact I am proud of it. Although, perhaps, undeserving of it I am glad that I furnished you with a suitable occasion to try your hand–or rather to manifest your, your–well, I will say, your marked attachment to me. I derive consolation in the reflection that an elegant and sensible woman never chides those who are not peculiarly dear to them. Pray do not think that vanity prompts this utterance; for it is the mere recital of a common place truism.

You ask me if I am "not a little bit obstinate?" I trust not. If I thought that there was such a quality in my nature I would war against it, with all my might, until it was utterly eradicated. While it is not a vicious, it is a mean passion–paralyzing to elevated character, if cordially indulged. I confess that in <u>purpose</u> I am <u>resolute</u>; in <u>principle</u> <u>unyielding</u>. When I have a noble aim to accomplish no earthly power can direct me from it. When I have a high duty to perform I can admit of no obstacle to its consummation. I may be impractical but I have a consciousness that I am consistent; and without rendering justice to that consciousness I should consider myself a heathen. As I never [fawned] to Vice in Purple so will I never turn against Virtue in Rags. In this sense I determined, from the first, to remain here, regardless of dear and new attachments, from the beginning to the end—enduring all, risking all, for humanity's sake. I had identified my fortunes with France six years ago and I would have been a renegade in my own estimation if I had fled from her in her hour of supreme trial. In all her [united] history there is no epoch of such wondrous, thrilling, interest as that of the rise, and duration, and fall of the <u>Commune</u>. It casts even the "Reign of Terror" into dim shade.

In the retrospect I shall fail to make you understand how much I rejoice that I was permitted to be a spectator and a sojourner. The population was reduced during the mobocratic rule to 500,000 or 600,000. The more opulent families affrighted well-nigh out of their senses, had managed to escape beyond the fortifications. Most of the orderly inhabitants who remained were seized with fear, which gradually increased to despair. The shops were as good as closed. A door here and there, half open, was the only indication that they were tenanted. Women and children were their only representatives. The able bodied men, under the threat of impressment into the ranks of the <u>Commune</u>, had absconded. I was in the center of the city—outdoors from morning till night; and, I fancied, from my venerable appearance, and composed bearing, and smoothing words, that I imparted comfort to many a sad soul. I thus felt that it was God's Will that I should be here; to administer to the surrounding care and sorrow, and in that sacred belief I had not a solitary thought of danger personal to myself. In such a duty if it were to die it were to die most gloriously and most happily. Will you not, My Dear Sweet Heart, with this explanation, which is far from covering the whole ground, pardon me for that which you may have deemed a foolhardy expression or a needless intrepidity? You need not, however, for I have in your unselfish virtues, as displayed throughout our own death struggles, an ample assurance of your forgiveness.

Irresistible as would be the <u>inducement</u>, under different circumstances, I cannot make up my mind to visit a land which is under the rule, and in political fellowship, with Yankeedom. When the South fell I took a vow that I would never more enter it, unless it should rise again. In the vicissitudes of the earth, under the operations of the Almighty's just laws, this will, sooner or later, inevitable occur.

Until then I must remain faithful to myself. My fidelity has already cost me much anguish of heart It may cost me many more pangs, but to suffer for a duty or an inflexible sentiment, if necessary, is an obligation imposed upon a Christian and a Philosopher—to be [variant] to "the still small voice within" would be to be false to the Divinity which inspires me. I want to serve the <u>cause</u> which "is not dead but sleepeth" by my example, to make, from day to day, sympathizers with it in Central Europe; so that when a propitious hour arrives I can enlist influential friends in its interest. I, if no one else, have <u>submitted</u> to nothing, <u>accepted</u> nothing, <u>Northern</u>. If through the perilous hours which I have passed the hoisting of the hated "Stars and stripes" would have shielded my life, my whole soul would have revolted at such a sacrifice of principle for so selfish an end. For a period of six months, or more, every foreigner in Paris had a Flag unfolded from his window except myself. That emblem which once victoriously floated over "the men in grey" was with me still—one of exceeding beauty bestowed upon me by my daughter-in-law when she was here, the work of her own hands. It was constantly spread over my bed, with my card upon it containing the words "I would prefer death under it to life under the Yankee Ensign. Should I succumb let my mortal remains rest beneath its honored folds." Nor had I my Passport but my Old Confederate one, as Commissioner, with the Pontifical and French [visas] of 1863. With this long explanation I fancy you will be convinced that I ought not to derogate from the high position which I at first assumed and have so consistently maintained.

Paris is again gay. The Boulevards are crowded and the Hotels crammed and jammed with the curious from around and from afar. In the ruins of a number of her splendid edifices there is an attraction which ever the Exhibition of 1867 did not present. Order is perfectly re-established and confidence as large as at any time under the [base-born]–Pardon! I forgot our agreement–Empire.[149] Look at the result yesterday of the new loan. 400,000,000 of dollars were needed and in a single day double that amount was subscribed! No country in Europe has such credit. If I read rightly the signs, the

---

149 This word, which appears to be "base-born," is likely Mann's derogatory term for Louis Napoleon.

day of revenge upon Prussia, strengthened by strong alliances, is not five years distant. "Wonderful People" as Washington designated them in 1796–more "Wonderful," still, now than then.[150] I cannot tear myself away from them for a sojourn at Como or Rome. I may remark that there were not exceeding 25,000 native Frenchmen engaged, with a heart intent, in the insurrection. All the rest were of foreign-birth, the rogues and assassins of every land.

I will try to get you the information which you desire from Clermont. I have a friend who would furnish me with every particular, a native of the Department of Puy-de-Dome, but he is absent, and has been since the commencement of the war. Auvergne is one of the most primitive regions of "La Belle France." [151]

I am really distressed on account of the delicacy of your health and the depression of your spirits, as stated in your Letter. In your next, which I shall soon expect in recognition of mine of the first of the month, I am hopeful that I shall be informed of your complete restoration. The climate of Carolina is one of the most enervating in creation, particularly to females. As it enfeebles the system so it eventually undermines the constitution, and operates deleteriously upon the mind. Oh! that you could, in view of your duties and interests, flee away from it to Europe, and here, or at Como and Milan, or Rome, be, with dear Anna, at rest from distracting care forever. Such a consummation would fill to the brim my cup of happiness.

I admire your love of "independence", and approve your determination not to separate with it; and the more so because of the unlikelihood that you would ever be suitably matched. Young maidens may marry beneath them, and raise by their excellence of character, their husbands up to their standard, eventually; but she who has been an idolized wife must seek her equal in heart and mind, (if she have no superior) in high qualities. Compatibility in all respects, in wedded life is the most difficult of attainment.

---

150 In a letter to French ambassador Pierre Adet dated January 1, 1796, George Washington praised the French and referred to them as a "Wonderful people!"

151 Clermont-Ferrand is a city in the Puy-de-Dome department of the Auvergne-Rhone-Alpes region of France.

"Love's young dream" impels the millions to Hymen's Altar, but alas! how few imbued with the importance of harmonious, and lasting, compatibility. You are a greater woman than you imagine yourself, too great for the companion of a man who has not eminent qualities of goodness and intellectual accomplishments. You have been gifted with a near genius. There are flashes in your correspondence that would have done credit to Byron, thoughts that breathe expressed in words that impress. All you needed was a suitable superior in which to move to become renowned in the esteem of the intelligent world. Believe me I pray you when I tell you this. I have no motive to flatter; nor would I, much as I prize, any more flatter even you than I would "flatter Neptune for his Trident or Jove for his power to Thunder." [152]

Thus estimating you–an estimate inaugurated by your Letters written seven year ago–my sympathizing heart turned at once to your lacerated one and pity opened its long sealed portals to a fresh affection which has been of incessant augmentation. It was not <u>Love</u> in the common acceptation of the word, not a passion engendered by personal charms. It was something more sublime, aye more holy, than that proceeding from such an emotion. It was the <u>spiritual, the eternal</u>; not of earth or of earth's emanation. I need not add that in all its original purity and all its force it still exists, nurtured by a mysterious supernatural agency–the very charm of my life. Although so many years your senior I fear to trust myself in the presence of your captivating person, lest it may assume a different character, one antagonistic to the exaltation of that which is so sacredly, and so unselfishly, (as concerns mortal passion and desire) [bears]. I could associate with you in this or other lands with safety, where there is so much for the mind to dwell upon, but in Charleston the reverse might occur. I might there <u>Love as your pair of suitors Love</u>, and then the Beautiful Ideal of Heaven would disappear in the Ugly Reality of Earth. I may not, without breaking the "Golden Cup" risk the experiment, were even no other considerations to influence me in not responding to your gracious request, "<u>I am waiting</u>."[153]

---

152 A quote from Shakespeare's *Coriolanus*.
153 This may be a reference to the "golden bowl" mentioned in Ecclesiastes 12:6, which may symbolize the head, and therefore, one's life.

Pray take good care of Anna's health. Patiently instruct her in all that is good and useful. Try and get into a mountainous district for the warm months. Let her breathe in the fresh morning air freely, and skip unrestrainedly over hill and dale. Be yourself to her at all times and she will ever be like yourself. The wisest of old has given the assurance "as the mother so will the daughter be." It is questionable whether, <u>in the man</u>, it is well that it should be so, but so it is nevertheless.

I am glad that you found "The Lost Principle." [154] Take care of it until there is a chance for its safe transmission. It will be most valuable to me in facts and dates.

Cheer up! Cheer up! Look hopefully to the future, and draw upon your own inexhaustible resources of intellect for reasonable joy and ample contentment.

Ever as Ever, your Devoted Affectionate Admirer,

        Dudley Mann

---

154 *The Lost Principle: or, The Sectional Equilibrium,* was a book by "Barbarossa" (a pen name for John Scott, 1820-1907), published in 1860.

Ambrose Dudley Mann, 17 Boulevard de la Madeleine, Paris, to Mrs. Laurence M. Keitt, Bennettsville, Marlboro District, S.C.

14 July 1871

My Ever Darling Friend: -

Your last, too short but oh! how sweet! Letter of June 22-24 was received yesterday. My mind is relieved with respect to your health, for you write as if it had never been impaired. Moreover you are cheerful, and if not actively contented, wisely philosophical. Need I say that I am not happy when assured by your own hand that you are not so? I should be unworthy of myself were it otherwise, and, therefore, unworthy of that never ceasing interest which animates you for my welfare.

My mind is at last made up to become a Citizen for "La Belle France." I have been a cosmopolitan, as respects nationality, ever since I lost my country. I could not consent to become a renegade to the principles of my birth, my education and my affection, by swearing allegiance to a Monarch. I can so swear with a hearty good will to a Republican such as Mr. Thiers and his well-intentioned co-adjutors are honestly resolved to durably found. I expect to be joyously received, and I hope to be eminently useful in the consummation of the great work. In this thought I have a new political existence and an attendant laudable ambition.

I utterly despair of the South. She is faithless to an honorable future, faithless to the noble "men in grey" who fought, and bled, and died for her. I perceive by the newspapers that she is disposed to accept the "New Departure" Platform of the Democrats of the North, which confirms all the Amendments to the Constitution by which she is enslaved.[155] Nothing as monstrous in public dishonesty ever occurred in any country as this vile abandonment of principle to secure place. It is a virtual, indeed political, amalgamation with the [Distributives] who have ruled at Washington for ten years. The truth

---

155 The New Departure was a political strategy of the Democratic Party designed to enlarge its political base.

is, that there is no good in the North, politically, and very little in the South. The lust for office and the greed for gain, through corrupt governmental influences, overpower every elevating sentiment. Virtue is in tears at the degrading spectacle.

I am pressed to-day by my engagements; but I could not let the French steamer go off without an expression of my gratitude for your truly affectionate Letter. Pray continue to write fortnightly. Tell me frankly all that is uppermost in your mind. It will be confined to a heart that is ever in sympathy with your own. Tell the two [Consuls] as <u>much</u> as you see fit, but tell me <u>every</u> thing. I am by right, not Divine, but of your own choosing, your Confessor.

Ah! how indeed I wish the "Mamma and Anna"–you put the latter first but I choose, for reasons personal to myself, to put her last–were with me in my nice little *<u>menage</u>*. I fancy that you would mightily enjoy the novelty of the change; and I am certain your presence would cure me of whatever there is of <u>selfishness</u> in my nature. What feasts of reason we should have, at any rate, I, in our <u>tete-a-tete</u> conversations. Anna would listen and learn. We would agree to have no secrets from her. I like your "<u>badinage</u>"as you term it. Favor me with more when you are in the humour. I presume I have received <u>all</u> your Letters which preceded that which arrived yesterday, and I doubt not that you are in possession of <u>all</u> mine. What a correspondence! I dare say you have written more to me than you ever wrote to any one else. I think I can say you have written more to me that you ever wrote to anyone else. I think I can say as much as concerns yourself. There had been a gap in my intellectual life in its absence. If some captivating wooer should charm you off, upset that resolution of yours "never to surrender your personal independence"—what would become of me? Echo answers <u>What</u>!

With kisses to Anna and as much love to yourself as is agreeable, or desirable, believe me your affectionately attached

Ambrose Dudley Mann

[P.S.] What scenes in New-York! ¹⁵⁶ How consoling the reflection that God made the country and Man made the city! ¹⁵⁷ Every thing at which the latter has tried his hand is more or less, faulty. Of this, exemplifications are abundant.

---

156 The "Orange Riots" took place in New York in July 1871.
157 A quote from the English poet and hymnodist William Cowper (1731-1800), who wrote that "God made the country, and man made the town."

Ambrose Dudley Mann, 17 Boulevard de la Madeleine, Paris, to Mrs. Laurence M. Keitt, Bennettsville, Marlboro District, S.C.

3 September 1871

Mon Tres Cher Ami:

Your most charming Letter, commenced on the 16t July and completed on the 3rd of August, was received a week ago. Its recognition would have been more prompt but for my wish to obtain some accurate information with respect as the matter which you so specially present to my consideration. As yet I am unsuccessful in my inquiries I, however, have mentioned, in terms of high commendation, to two personages, who enjoy the confidence of the Government of Versailles, the name of your friend in connection with the post at New-York, who promised me to bring it before the proper Department at the earliest auspicious moment. I understand that it is in contemplation to change the active consular system of France, which is believed to be singularly defective in salutary operation. All new appointments will, probably, be superinduced by <u>political</u> motives. <u>Patronage</u> will be employed to strengthen <u>Administration</u>; or, to speak more plainly, "the spoils" will be parceled out "to the victors." While, indirectly, I will exert myself to serve you I cannot approach Mr. Thiers upon the subject nor any member of his Cabinet. My relations with the United States preclude such a procedure. It would be to manifest an interest in them were I to ask for an appointment to one of their ports; and might be regarded as a friendly acknowledgement of their disgraceful existence. The most I can do is, is the manner indicated, shielding myself behind <u>your</u> recommendation.

Pray, let me, My Darling Friend, define more clearly, than ever before, my <u>true</u> position. I stand here as I have stood in Europe since I entered the service of the Confederate States, as an <u>alien</u>, to all intents and purposes, to the Federal Government. When I became a Plenipotentiary of these States I expatriated myself from the Union. Henceforward I was no more a Citizen of it than I was of China. I withdrew from its protection and covered myself with a Flag unstained by crime, as pure in origin as it was honest in purpose.[158] Its suppression by brutal force served but to increase its virtues in my esteem. The idol of my affections in its glorious career it has become the idol of my devotions in its silent obscurity. It has no representative in Europe, (I say its not in a boasting spirit), who has been so faithful to it as myself. I could not, ever were an evil genius to endeavor to impel me, do otherwise than remain so, however long my life may be protracted. I want by my example, to impress confidence and <u>constancy</u> upon the rising question of the South, and to furnish convincing proof to the public rule of Europe that there is at least one Confederate had that never quailed, that never relinquished a just <u>principle</u> to benefit a selfish <u>interest</u>, that never despaired to eventual public justice. In my private chamber I considered myself quite as much the representative of the noble souls existing, as well as departed of the South as I did when I was honored <u>officially</u> with the high trust bestowed upon me. All my colleagues are gone; the two first, Mr. Yancey[159] and Mr. Rost[160], went first; the last two, Mr. Mann and Mr. Slidell went last. <u>They all thoroughly knew my inexorable resolution never to surrender</u>. It has pleased the blessed Redeemer to preserve me, and I am inspired by Him to think that it was for an <u>object</u>. That object in due time, I have an abiding belief, will develop itself. When a propitious hour arrives the story of my humble life will, I trust, produce its valuable fruits. I cannot explain to you the <u>modus operandi</u>, for the redemption of the South but I am certain that the plea has been [definitively avenged] by Almighty Wisdom.[161] Since the coming of our Saviour the civilized globe has not been in such a peculiar state of transition. In its rule that which would have been considered as a miracle ten years ago

---

158 The Second Confederate National Flag (used from 1863 to the end of the war) was also known as the Stainless Banner.

159 William Lowndes Yancey (1814-1863) of Alabama was the Confederate commissioner for England and France.

160 Pierre Adolph Rost (1797-1868) was the commissioner of the Confederate States of America for Spain. A native of France, he immigrated to Louisiana in 1816.

161 In 1881, Mann wrote to Davis, "The perfidy of the North to the South is sure to be overtaken by the vengeance of Heaven." Mann, *"My Ever Dearest Friend,"* 69.

is now viewed as a reasonable reality. In human affairs there is no longer any thing, of occurrence, to excite wonder. Read, I beseech you, this paragraph over again and lay it by for a future perusal.

I may remark of your last Letter that you never wrote one which so thrilled me with joyous emotion. I like your magnanimity to your discarded lover. In it is to be found the very essence, in refined concentration, of feminine greatness and goodness. I should despise myself if I were capable of <u>jealousy</u>. I never knew anything of that ignoble passion; nor have I ever had a particle of <u>envy</u> in my nature. They are kindred spirits, the offspring of base born minds. Ought I not, (as I assuredly am) to be very proud of your emphatic declaration that "<u>There</u> <u>are</u> <u>no</u> <u>[turns]</u> <u>in</u> <u>your</u> <u>path</u>." What an honor, what a consolation! This alone is glory enough to satisfy my highest aspirations. I have no nobler ambition than to forever merit this cordial preference. I rejoice that you have last broken with your rigid reserve, and opened to your best friend on earth, your heart so freely and fully. I beg you to always so write. Two such souls as ours should, in their intercourse, be under no restraint of thought.

Anna I hope is growing in wisdom and knowledge; and all else that can gratify your wishes and expectations. In your precepts give her the full benefit of your example. Kiss her lovingly for me.

I read your handwriting with familiar ease. How do you manage with mine? so curious and difficult. Pray why do you not favor me, fortnightly, with a Letter?! Believe me always yours with the most devoted affection,

A. Dudley Mann

Ambrose Dudley Mann, 51 Rue de Luxembourg, Paris, to Mrs. Susan Sparks Keitt, Bennettsville, S.C.[162]

18 June 1874

My Dear Mrs. Keitt:

Your Letter mailed at New York May 28, and dated along in March, has just been received. I have been for so many tedious months without tidings from you that I was almost in despair of ever hearing from you again, in your own hand writing.

Oh! that I should be so far form you, and so powerless for the soothing of your manifold griefs. I had ventured to indulge the hope that instead of an increase in their magnitude the cause of their existence had been measurable, if not totally, removed. Sad, sad indeed, is the fate of poor South Carolina. History scarcely furnishes an instance of a Commonwealth having been subjected to such fiendish wrongs as you so forcibly portray. But alas! I must feebly own that I see not a ray of hope for their redress as long as the negro is <u>supreme</u>; and how long that will be passeth my understanding. It must be years–it may be ages.

The reasons which you assign for not employing <u>Agents</u> are as explicit as they are otherwise shocking. What can you do to better yourself in view of the prevailing untrustworthiness? Unhappily I can suggest nothing. Your own judgment, dictated to by the force of imperious circumstances, as events arrive, will likely not be in error. How hard that one so worthy of Heaven's choicest blessings should have undergone such schooling in adversity's severities! Still this nether world is made up of strange things, ever running into contradictory extremes. But that "there is a Divinity which shapes our ends" mysteriously and wisely I would be inclined to think that the creation of human being was a misconception.

With respect to Dear Anna the thought of her absence from school would be an afflicting one were I not consoled with the confident

---

[162] The envelope for this letter is addressed to "Mrs. Susan Sparks Keitt (of Mandeville), Bennettsville, South Carolina (Darlington District)."

belief that her future, for goodness, and usefulness, is incalculably better assured by your presence to her, that the presence of any other instructress, however accomplished. With your daily example, she will, in emulating you, receive an education that will adorn her ever. She will learn enough to be ever wise, and ever self sustaining, in any circle which she may enter. I have ever pitied the girl that is sent off to a boarding-school to know the risk of a taint by Tom Boy companions, and heartless [miserly] mistresses, of the noble natural qualities of heart. It there is one institution or cult that I positively hate, of a co-called respectable nature, it is a Female Boarding School. Do Keep Anna with you and let her enjoy the full benefit of your society and your accomplishments, and her life will be one of pure innocence. A daughter who has as utterly worldly mother, or even a weak-minded one, may be severed from her with advantage, but she who has an unselfish, loving, intellectual one, never, no never.

Your devotion to your venerable excellent father is beyond all praise. Among the last words of our Saviour were those three touching ones to St. John: "Behold thy mother." Mary was advancing in year, and he meant that she should be cared for. It was addressed to the children of all time in the spirit of Heavenly thoughtfulness. "Behold Thy Father or Behold thy mother" in declining years is the holiest injunction ever imposed on sons and daughters, and that my dear good friend you have observed, and will observe to the last, with a fidelity never surpassed. Write to me, I beseech you, more frequently. By so doing you will relieve your heart from its sorrow. I never see the Perkins for the reason that I have no relations with them. I will explain why in a future letter. They have no family but her unmarried daughter, Miss Bayley. Very few Germans show their faces in Paris now-a-days, but I will try to learn something of the [Count] you mention. Mr. Davis, our President, has been here. He was with me a month, partaking of simple fare and sharing my apartment. We have been lifetime friends. May God bless you, My Dearest Friend, and fortify you for all the vexations to which you may be submitted, is the prayer of Your Affectionate Friend,

              Dudley Mann

Ambrose Dudley Mann, 51 Rue de Luxembourg, Paris, to Mrs. Susan Sparks Keitt, Bennettsville, S.C.[163]

10 December 1874

My Ever Dear Mrs. Keitt:

Have my Letters failed to reach you or have yours, in acknowledgement of them, failed to reach me? I know not; but I do know that from month to month, for full six, I have been in disappointed expectation of receiving one of your ever inestimable communications. – I try to console myself with the trite axiom that "no news is good news," and that yourself, and Anna, and your father, are in the enjoyment of excellent health, and as happy as you could reasonably expect to be in this world of cares and griefs.

The aspect of affairs in South Carolina, as I contemplate them at this distance, seem to me to be more assuring for the improvement of the material condition of the State than at any period since the termination of the war. The rebuke that Grant received in the recent elections, and the increasing sentiment in the North adverse to the encouragement of the negroes to preserve in hostility to their former masters, will, I think, soon eventuate in the restoration of <u>white</u> supremacy, even in the Old Palmetto Commonwealth. The political revolution, evidenced in the recent elections, is the most remarkable and momentous in its character that has ever occurred in the history of the Union, and in the belief that it will still be onward, I fancy that the day is not far away when the amendments to the Constitution, so unwarrantably adopted for the humiliation of the Confederate States, will be indignantly expunged therefrom. Under their operations <u>States</u> <u>Rights</u> can have no other than a mere nominal existence, and therefore the triumphant party in the late contest, which professes to be devoted to those Rights, has no alternative but to remove every hindrance to their salutary administration. In this view of the matter there is cause for us to be hopeful. [164]

---

163 This letter is addressed to Mrs. Keitt at Bennettsville, Darlington District.

164 In the elections of 1874, the Democrats secured a majority in the U.S. House of Representative for the first time since before the war.

I trust that under your special direction and noble daily example, Anna is progressing in useful personal accomplishments, and general intelligence, satisfactorily. Daily observation convinces me, more and more, that a daughter, in her earlier years, is ever better instructed by her mother, if she have a good one, than at a school; for that which she learns she learns as much from affection as from interest, and therefore the knowledge is durable and the inclination to improve it incessant. More of eloquence in manner and expression, and of practical information, is derived from conversation than from books.

Am I ever to see you? I begin to despair of this most desired of all earthly joys. Still I will not relinquish the hope altogether, for it would be to relinquish one of my most cherished pleasures.

If you should chance to see our good friend, Mr. Raymond pray be so obliging as to tell him of my profound thankfulness for his kind mindfulness in sending me occasionally the Charleston News.[165]

Paris is orderly, and as gay as I ever saw it as this season of the year. Oh! that you and Anna could be with me at Christmas, to enjoy its peculiar delights! It is so long since I have had tidings of you that you may be married, or going to be, and that this may be the cause of your continued silence.

Believe me always Your Affectionate Friend,

Ambrose Dudley Mann

---

165 This may have been Henry Hunter Raymond (1822-1876), a Charleston lawyer.

Ambrose Dudley Mann, Chantilly, France, to Mrs. Susan Keitt, Darlington District, S.C. c/o Mr. T. P. Lide[166]

4 May 1879

My Ever Dear Mrs. Keitt:

After so lengthened a suspension in your excellent correspondence you may imagine with that emotions of joy I hailed the arrival of your last charming letter.

I share your pride in the very brilliant conquests, of medals, achieved by your darling daughter in her graduation. They are trophies which will adorn her ever, and at the same time serve as testimonials to the careful manner in which you reared her from her infancy. However high your expectations of her progress to womanhood you enjoy the bliss of her having fully realized them, while she enjoys the delighting satisfaction that she was equal in performance to the grand accomplishments. Thus, you are especially worthy of each other. A worth, so founded, is of paradisiacal sublimity. It is of conscientious creation and commands the admiration of elevated humanity. It is purpose in purity, combined with intellectual perseverance, teaching mothers and daughters by example. Your darling, as relates to herself, leaves you nothing desire [sic] in her useful accomplishments. What a glorious consummation! Her future, I am quite confident will be in perfect accordance with it. How much I wish that you were both here I cannot express. This has become par excellence the gay region of "La Belle France." It is the rendezvous of the old nobility and rich gentry, for pleasure and for sport. The duc d'Aumale[167] has just rebuilt the old Chateau, demolished in 1793, at a cost of 6,000,000 francs. He is the wealthiest individual in France, and he is dispensing his income in the improvement of the celebrated Forest, on the Southern border of which I am located.[168] He is a childless

---
166 This letter is addressed from "Mon Repos: pres Chantilly" to Mrs. Keitt, care of T. P. Lide in Darlington, S.C. This was likely Thomas Park Lide (1810-1882), a relative of Mrs. Keitt.
167 Prince Henri d'Orleans, the Duc d'Aumale, rebuilt the Grand Chateau de Chantilly after it was burned during the French Revolution.
168 The Chantilly Forest, a large forest in the Oise department of France.

widower of 58, the commander of one of the six military divisions, and the first man, perhaps, in ability, in the nation; certainly the adorning jewel of all that remains of the House of the Bourbons. There are no, so to speak, <u>love matches</u> in France. The nobility, of both sexes, marry with an eye singular to the bettering of their pecuniary condition. Each requires a money consideration, and if that is available in sufficiency all else is easily arranged. Hence the <u>nouveau</u> <u>riche</u>, or <u>parvenus</u> are now marrying their children to those of the poor nobility with slender means. Thereby the one obtains entrance into the cream of society, while the other is furnished with resources for the gratification of enjoyments. If yourself and Anna were with me, I could introduce you to the first circles, and you could judge for yourselves. I have, as a neighbor, a young Viscount who can trace his blood back 500 years, and who has the entrance to the most <u>recherche</u> <u>salons</u> of Paris, who is inclined to marry an American lady, but a large dot [169] is a primary requisite, one of 25,000 francs a year. His own income is about 15,000. At the death of his Uncle, who is not far from four-score years, he will inherit the title of Count. He is too proud of his lineage to unite himself with a <u>nouveau</u> <u>riche</u> belle. I am fond of him, and he comes often to see me.

"Mathilde" and "[Rosine]" have been in Paris since December.[170] They are in the height of fashion, and have the wherewithal for its enjoyment. They return to their summer residence next month; to abide, but they make frequent flying visits to it.

I was prepared from his advanced age to hear of the death of your father. [171] It will ever be a source of consolation to you that you so tenderly and faithfully performed in the [extremest] sense your duty to your mother and himself.

---

169 Dowry.
170 "Mathilde" was likely Marguerite Mathilde d'Erlanger (1842-1927). The other name, which appears to be Rosine, may refer her sister Marie Rosine de St. Roman. Daughters of John Slidell, they married into French nobility.
171 Samuel Sparks died on September 19, 1878, at the age of 91.

The burning of your old historical mansion was a sad calamity. It robbed your estate of its crowning feature and yourself of treasured relics that can never be replaced. But Nature will have its hard ways whenever it chooses, and humanity cannot better help itself than in submission.

My "Work" is still in progress and will so continue, I presume, as long as I am able to wield a pen. I have had no time to write the sequel to Tammie Chattie. Dear old fellow, he is now sleeping soundly on a chair by my side. He is in his fourteenth years and more lovely than ever, in goodness and manner.

I am living in strictly rustic simplicity, in accordance with my tastes, a faithful observer of the motto of Apelles: "No day without a line." [172] I regret that I know not the address of Mr. Benjamin in London.[173] I have never been in correspondence with him. With much love to your angelic like daughter. I pray you to believe me your ever affectionate friend.

                Dudley Mann.

[Small note enclosed with above letter:]

May 5

I have just received a note from Miss Emily Mason, informing me of her return to Paris from the U.S., and that she is accompanied by two Miss Barnwells of S.C. She has brought as she says "a number of good things for me from old friends." I expect her here in a day or two, when she will post me up fully in relation to American affairs.

Your pecuniary embarrassments distress me all the more because of my utter inability to offer you the means for their removal. My securities in which I relied for perfect ease and independence are

---

172 Apelles, a painter of ancient Greece, was said to let no day pass without practicing his art.

173 Judah P. Benjamin (1811-1884) served in several Confederate cabinet offices, including that of the Secretary of State. After the war he went to England and practiced law there.

next to worthless, through the evil spirit of repudiation which has entered the Legislature of one of the Southern States, in which I had implicit confidence on the integrity of.

I hope that you will work through triumphantly and save Mandeville. Never despair. "God helps those who help themselves." It would be one of the happiest of my days that I could see you without a care. No human being ever deserved more such a blessing. But you are always rich in your daughter's excellence of character while nine out of every ten mothers are poor. Let this console you.

Pray write to me as soon as your convenience will permit. Your letters are the delight of my life. My gout stiffened fingers now and then prevent me from using my pen, except to <u>scratch</u> out along on my work in a manner not clear.

Again, believe me always

    Yours Affectionately

        A. Dudley Mann

Ambrose Dudley Mann, Chantilly, France, to Mrs. Susan Sparks Keitt of Mandeville

25 December 1882

The compliments of this joyous day to the Christian World, with the continued affectionate regards, and best wishes of

AMBROSE DUDLEY-MANN

I wrote to you some time in June last, informing you of the demise of my beloved daughter-in-law, since when I have not been favored with a letter from you. I long for tidings and those of the most gladdening nature, respecting yourself and Anna.[174]

---

174 This last communication from Mann was written on his calling card. His daughter-in-law Susan Cumming Mann died on May 4, 1882, and is buried in Savannah, Ga.

Epilogue

AMBROSE DUDLEY MANN, like all human beings, had his faults. He was perhaps quixotic in his devotion to a beautiful young widow who would always remain a distant, unrealized vision of happiness. Yet, as far as we know, he remained a true friend to her until his death, and he remained equally true to the principles to which he had dedicated his life. Honor, duty, and patriotism were foremost among those principles, and perhaps there is something to be learned from such a life.

In 1930, the famous English writer G. K. Chesterton published an essay entitled "On America." In it he asserted that, although the 20th century was the "Age of America," there was "a virtue lacking in the age, for want of which it will certainly suffer and possibly fail." That virtue, according to Chesterton, was honor, the idea of which was embodied in "the spirit of the Old South." The present-day world, he concluded, was crying out for this spirit, and desperately needed the "Southern gentleman."

> And we need the Southern gentleman more than the English or French or Spanish gentleman. For the aristocrat of Old Dixie, with all his faults and inconsistencies, did understand what the gentleman of Old Europe generally did not. He did understand the Republican ideal, the notion of the Citizen as it was understood among the noblest of the pagans. That combination of ideal democracy with real chivalry was a particular blend for which the world was immeasurably the better; and for the loss of which it is immeasurably the worse. It may never be recovered, but it will certainly be missed.

Appendix

Savannah *Morning News*, Sunday, August 16, 1896

THE LIFE OF A DIPLOMAT

Judge Mann to Write Memoirs of His Father, A. Dudley Mann

A History of Stirring Events—Unpublished Details of Inner Workings of the Confederacy—Peep into Court Circles of Europe. Written by an ex-Savannahian

A volume of memoirs is now being prepared in Chicago, the publication of which will, beyond all question, attract international attention and arouse students of recent American history to a profound degree.

Over six years have passed since the death of A. Dudley Mann, the diplomat who negotiated the first reciprocity treaty for the United States, the Assistant Secretary of State under President Buchanan and the first diplomatic commissioner of the confederacy to the European powers. Just before he died at his beautiful country home in France, and when he was over 90 years of age, he placed in the hands of his son, Judge W. Grayson Mann of Chicago, the biographical and historical data covering, in minute detail, his whole remarkable career, but stipulating that the memoirs must not be published within six years after his death. This limitation has expired and consequently the almost untouched field of the diplomatic history of the confederate states will receive an invaluable addition from the rich experiences of the man who was trusted with one of the most important state secrets of the Buchanan administration and of the Jefferson Davis regime.

The Hon. Wilson [sic] Grayson Mann is well remembered as a former and prominent citizen of Savannah. He lived here for many years. His wife, the only daughter of the late G. B. Cummings of this city, died in Italy, which country she was visiting about fifteen years ago. Mr. Mann then removed to Florida, and afterwards to Chicago. Of himself and his book the Chicago Evening Post says:

The peculiar fitness of Judge Mann for the loving labor of editing the mass of letters, documents and memoranda placed in his hands by his father lies not only in his skill and experience as a writer, but also in the fact that he began to act as interpreter to the elder diplomat early in his teens, later became his private secretary, and was his constant companion through all the varied scenes and on all important public missions which engaged his years in activity. In addition to this wide experience, Judge Mann was, for a considerable period, secretary to James M. Mason, who was sent, with John Slidell, to represent the confederacy in England and France, and whose capture, while on board the English Trent, by Capt. Charles Wilkes, almost precipitated war between England and the United States. He was also selected by President Buchanan as one of two representatives sent by this government into Mexico, on a secret mission, to prepare a report upon which the United States based its action in recognizing the governing body of that country, then in the throes of disruption as a consequence of Louis Napoleon's far-reaching and crafty plans of conquest.

The elder Mann was a Virginian of the Virginians. His aristocratic birth, his natural talents and an early mastery of law, especially in the constitutional branches, combined to place him in a position of political prominence in the old dominion state when a young man. Virginia then exercised an almost dominating influence in the politics of the nation, and the future diplomat soon found himself a favorite in the administration circles at Washington. The death of his wife, when their only son was an infant, resulted in making the relationship between father and son one of peculiar intimacy and tenderness. They were seldom or never absent from each other, and this constant companionship led the son to regard his father more as a friend and comrade than as the embodiment of parental authority. Nearly all of Judge Mann's education was obtained from tutors in the various cities of continental Europe, where he obtained in boyhood a wide command of the modern European languages and a thorough knowledge of the customs and social usages of the countries in which he traveled with his father.

When, in 1846, his father was appointed minister plenipotentiary and envoy extraordinary to the thirty-nine smaller German states, his linguistic attainments were so marked that he was selected to act as interpreter, although he was but 14 years of age. It was while engaged in this mission that A. Dudley Mann established with the states of Hanover, Oldenburg and Mecklenburg what are undoubtedly entitled to go down in history as the first reciprocity treaties made by this government. President Buchanan so regarded them and took a keen personal interest and pride in their establishment.

Those earliest days of the boy's introduction to public service as his father's interpreter covered a period of great political disturbance and unrest on the continent, and he naturally found himself at the very centers of excitement.

"I well remember," said Judge Mann, as he sat in his home in Grand boulevard, last night, surrounded by a mass of letters by scores of the last half-century, "the stirring scenes of those days. They made a sharp impression upon my boyish susceptibilities and I understood just enough of their deeper significance to enter thoroughly into the spirit of them. One of the most exciting scenes of this kind that came within my personal observation was the episode which practically set rolling the ball of the German revolution."

"At that time we were stationed at Munich, the capital of Bavaria, then under the corrupt court of old King Louis. While he was nominally King of Bavaria, that country was practically subject to the whim of Lola Montes, a notorious favorite of his court. To increase the resources of his exchequer, upon which his profligate expenditures made heavy demands, a tax upon beer was levied. This was the last straw upon the backs of the people. They looked upon Lola Montes as the government and the author of their hardships."

"Groups of peasants, working people and students congregated at street corners, about the public squares and public-houses and discussed their grievances. Just four days before the outbreak of the revolution in Paris I saw her carriage driving along Maximilian strasse. A band of students had become involved in a melee which threatened to develop into a riot. She was a bold, daring woman, and as soon as her carriage came up to the contestants, she pushed open the door, sprang out, evidently with the purpose of restoring order. But the effect of her appearance was like throwing a firebrand into a thatch of dry flax. There was a quick movement among the rioters and a butcher of Herculean proportions pushed aside his companions, rushed forward to the king's favorite and threw his arms about her. For a moment it seemed that she would be crushed, but the timely arrival of assistance enabled her to break from his grasp and take refuge in a neighboring church. She was subsequently removed in safety from her hiding place, but her reign—for It practically amounted to that—was at an end, and she was soon banished from Bavaria."

In June, 1849, the father received instructions from his home government to proceed to Vienna and investigate the Hungarian revolution under the leadership of Kossuth, with a view to a recognition of the latter by the United States. The fall of Kossuth's cause, through the inexplainable surrender of Gorgey, about two months after the Manns arrived in Vienna, put an end to this mission, but resulted in a life friendship between the Hungarian hero and the then minister of this government. Their subsequent correspondence was of the most intimate nature, and Judge Mann has many letters written to his father in the dashing liberator's own hand.

A. Dudley Mann was the first minister of this government sent to the Republic of Switzerland and was assistant secretary of state under William L. Marcy.

It is in the story of his appointment as the first commissioner of the confederacy, his association with Yancey, Rost, Mason and Slidell, the commissioners subsequently sent abroad, and the secret negotiations which he conducted with the great statesmen, and with the pope, that the greatest interest centers.

"When the provisional congress of the confederacy met at Montgomery," said Judge Mann, "I was a citizen of New Orleans and went forward with the Louisiana delegation as a secretary. My father was, of course, at Washington. At that time I was determined to secure a commission in the southern army. Mr. Davis was inaugurated Feb. 18, 1861, and I attended his first levee, which was held at the hotel, immediately after those ceremonies.

"As I joined the line of these who were greeting Mr. Davis as the first president of the confederacy, he drew me aside and asked:

"'Where is your father?'

"'In Washington,' I answered.

"'Telegraph him immediately to-night that I appoint him the first commissioner of the confederacy to represent it abroad.'

"Then he talked with me in relation to my own plans and purposes. I wished to secure a commission in the army, but he said there were many to go to the front, while very few had an experience like my own which would render them invaluable in connection with the diplomatic service.

"I followed out his instructions and at the very hour when the message was received at my father's hotel he was at the white house, whither he had been summoned by President Buchanan. The cabinet was then in session and my father was invited into the conference and informed that, although it was well known that his sympathies were with the south, the confidence of the chief executive and his official advisers in my father's integrity and loyalty was such as to influence them to request him to undertake a most important mission to England. The he was told that in the brief time before Mr. Buchanan must give place to Abraham Lincoln, it had been determined to secure, if possible, the good offices of Queen Victoria as a mediator between the north and south, hoping thereby to avoid bloodshed. He was informed that his letters of credit were ready; that brief instructions had already been drawn up by the Secretary of State and that he must come to an immediate decision in order to embark upon his journey that night.

"His reply was he must have a few moments for reflection—and with that answer of indecision he returned to his hotel. There he found awaiting him my message, sent at the request of Mr. Davis. His sympathies with the south were too strong to be resisted and he immediately signified his acceptance of the mission offered by the confederacy and notified President Buchanan of an unfavorable decision regarding the latter's request.

"Two other commissioners, the brilliant and eloquent William L. Yancey and Judge Alfred B. Rost, were also named by Mr. Davis a commissioners of the confederacy to the European powers and at his personal appointment I was made secretary to my father, who had sailed for England without delay, arriving there May 20, 1861, about two weeks in advance of the other commissioners and the secretaries.

"Affairs moved very slowly until the autumn of 1861 and it was difficult to obtain any satisfaction from Lord Palmerston, then premier, or from Earl Russell, the foreign secretary. Perhaps the most important thing which my father accomplished was to secure the friendship of Sir Evelyn Ashley, a nephew of Palmerston. He was closely in touch with the latter and kept us informed regarding the interests of our cause, so far as his uncle's attitude was concerned, to the extent that he could without any violation of confidence or infraction of the ethics of honor.

"But suddenly our sky became bright with hope! The return of Mr. Yancey and Judge Rost to America in order to assume other duties became necessary, and James M. Mason of Virginia and John Slidell of Louisiana were appointed to succeed them as commissioners.

They were captured by Capt. Charles Wilkes while they were on their way to England on board the British mail steamer Trent, and were taken to Fort Warren, in Boston harbor.

"I shall never forget the day when the news of this episode reached London. The excitement was terrific and Lord Palmerston was enraged. Through his most trusted channel of information the word came to my father that the prime minister had himself penned a message as bitter and insulting as a diplomatic note could be, had called a meeting of his cabinet and stated that if it were not sustained and forwarded he would resign.

"At that moment it seemed almost certain to the struggling representative of the confederacy that an undreamed-of stroke of Providence had intervened in behalf of his cause and that the United States would certainly be called upon to carry on a war with England at the same time that she was fighting to put down the rebellion. That the end of such a complication was certain victory to the confederacy my father could not doubt.

"Palmerston's warlike note, however, had to go to the queen for her approval. This, however, was considered a mere matter of form. When it came back from her it was changed from a practical declaration of hostilities to a polite and conciliatory message. Her majesty and many of those nearest her held strong anti-slavery sentiments and she, perhaps for the first and only time of her life, exercised the prerogative of an absolute monarch, dictated the spirit and letter of a diplomatic communication which held the fate of a war in its phraseology, and practically, defied the will of the premier of the British people. More than that, it is not too much to think that her determined stand against her prime minister also decided the fate of the confederate states of America, for with the intense feeling already existing in England and America there could have been but one result from Palmerston's savage note. The congress of the United States had thanked Capt. Wilkes for his capture of Mason and Slidell, the people of both countries were in a frenzy and Palmerston was excited to the verge of rage. He went so far as to make active preparations for war and my father was informed that the plan was to hold Quebec and to center all the naval force about the Chesapeake, where it could support Lee's army, making Baltimore and Washington its objective points.

"I am not aware that the remarkable course of Queen Victoria in this matter has ever been made public before, and it is interesting to speculate upon whether she could to-day override the foreign policy of a prime minister by the exercise of her monarchial mandate and will as she did then.

"Those days of waiting for this diplomatic complication to come to an end were days of the most tremendous strain and excitement to the commissioner of the confederacy, as well as to his son and secretary. But the queen's determined action in softening the note to the United States government, and the cautious and politic course of Secretary Seward in avoiding the great responsibility of a war with England, led to the pacific adjustment of the matter by the surrender of Mason and Slidell, who were allowed to go on their mission and joined my father in London. Slidell went to Paris, and Mason remained in England, where he received marked attention from many aristocratic families.

"One day he came to our rooms and announced that he had received an invitation to spend a week with the marquis and marchioness of Bath. He was a polished gentleman, according to the free and easy standard of Virginia, but he was shrewdly conscious that the requirements of the British nobility were of a different character.

"'Yes, suh! They've invited me, suh! And I wish to accept,' he said to my father. 'You know more about how things are done ovah heah, and I wish you to advise me. Will you do so, suh?'

"'Certainly,' answered my father. 'In the first place I would say you should stop chewing, and in the next place you must secure a valet, a body servant. No gentleman travels here without a valet.'

"He took the advice in good nature, and secured the services of a long-jointed and awkward fellow called John and went to the house of his aristocratic host. When he returned my father inquired:

"'Well, senator, how did you enjoy yourself with the English aristocracy?'

"'Nevah had such an experience in muh life, suh—nevah! At the dinnah they all showed me marked attention and wished to know all about the confederacy. The ladies were beautiful and charming, but I was glad when they arose and left the gentlemen to their cigars. Not that I wanted a cigar! What is a cigar, suh, to a man who has chewed several hogsheads of the old Virginia tobacco—and then suddenly finds himself cut off from that comfort? Only the great Creator knows how mightily I wanted a chaw just at the minute!'

"'I had taken the precaution to slip a small plug into the pocket of my wescut, but I had regard to your instructions, suh, and I waited until the gentlemen had finished their cigars and started to join the ladies. By that time I wanted a chaw so bad I slipped out of the door to the gallery that surrounded the house. It was raining slightly, but I didn't mind that. A little way out in the yard was a small saplin' which stood in the shadow. I ran to that, threw one arm about it, and with the other hand drew the plug from my pocket and pushed the whole of it into my mouth at once. May the confederacy be whipped to blazes, suh, if anything ever tasted so good to me in all my life as that did! You know that there's sand in the tobacco of Virginia, suh, and I've chawed so much of it that my teeth are worn off like the legs of Munchausen's dogs.'

"Senator Slidell was older and more cool, cunning and calculating than Senator Mason. He was the political Warwick of Louisiana and had attained prominence in the United States Senate, as had Mr. Mason. The latter was hot-blooded, impetuous and fiery in his patriotism. The difference in temperament between the two was well illustrated by an incident which occurred when they were prisoners at Fort Warren. They were put in underground cells. Mr. Slidell, who had a wonderful command of the vocabulary of expletives, completely exhausted it on that occasion, and then turning to his distinguished colleague in misery, said:

"'Mr. Mason, I believe they want to kill us.'

"Without a moment's hesitation Mason replied:

"'Kill us? I hope to the great God that they will, suh! That is the one thing that will make a triumphant confederacy, and I hope they will kill us!'

"During the first part of their confinement in the fort they were treated with considerable favor and were allowed eight drinks a day, but later they came under the general discipline of the prison and their potations were cut down to one drink a day. This allowance was handed in through a small window, and Mr. Mason told us that for two hours before the appointed time for the cupbearer to appear the prisoners would gather before this window and talk of nothing save the expected liquor, its poor quality and the insufficiency of its quantity.

The only personal interview with a sovereign which the elder Mann conducted was with Pope Pius IX, by whom he was received in the throne room and with much pomp and ceremonial. The Swiss guards were present and the pope sat upon his throne, listened to the address of the representative of the confederacy, who said that the priesthood of the south believed that an epistle from his holiness, urging reconciliation between the north and south implying that he would consent to act as mediator, might be productive of much good. Pius IX said that he would write a letter, and did so, but Louis Napoleon refused to permit its publication in the official paper of his court. This was in 1863.

"Although my father had a beautiful county seat in one of the most magnificent forests of France, he spent much time in Paris and was caught there by the siege. While the people about him were eating rats he was feasting upon American canned goods—and all because he chanced to have in his cellar three large casks of very fine and old brandy! Among his intimate acquaintances was a wholesale grocer, who had, just before the siege, received an importation of canned goods from America. But fine brandy was meat as well as drink to the old grocer, and herein was my father's strength. The latter would take a flask of his old brandy, take it to the grocer and receive in exchange a can of food. In this way he lived much more comfortably than the starving wretches about him, although he was obliged to be very secret about it. One day, through United States Minister Washburne, he received a note from a friend, which informed him that a large Virginia ham had been left with the concierge at the friend's establishment, and that my father could obtain it by presenting the note.

"You may be sure that he lost no time In going to the concierge and demanding the ham. He was met with tears and apologies, and for a few minutes thought that his hunger was to be unsatisfied and that the old concierge and his wife had devoured the ham. At last the wife recovered from her penitential grief sufficiently to explain that they had been forced by hunger to devour one small side of the Virginia delicacy. Father seized the ham, gave them his willing forgiveness and returned to his apartments, more delighted than he would have been with the possession of a gold mine. The ham lasted forty-one days, and was served in an almost innumerable variety of forms. He said that he never before knew the capabilities of ham."

In January, 1859, Judge Mann was sent by President Buchanan as a secret envoy to Mexico. He was accompanied by William Churchwell, and they were to report upon the condition of affairs in Mexico, as United States Senator Sam Houston had made a strong plea for the establishment by the United States of a protectorate over the land of the cactus. They started out with letters of credit, a plentiful assortment of good clothing, a pair of Winchesters and two large Colt's navy revolvers. At Vera Cruz they were cautioned to leave everything of value behind them, as they might be robbed. But they scorned this advice—and were stripped of everything before they reached the city of Mexico.

Fortunately, Judge Mann secreted his letters of credit underneath his collar, which was attached to his shirt. They were therefore able to obtain a new outfit of respectable clothing. But before they reached the coast they had again been robbed five times, and, on one occasion, the gentlemanly bandit who acted as master of ceremonies forced Judge Mann to interpret his demands to the English-speaking passengers of the coach in which they were riding. Their experience greatly amused President Buchanan, who paid their losses out of a secret fund at his disposal. The result of the mission was the recognition of the Juarez anti-aristocratic party of Mexico.

The publication of the memoirs of Dudley Mann, edited by Judge Mann, will be looked forward to with keen anticipation by all who are interested in the diplomatic history of the confederacy.

Bibliography

Manuscripts

John S. Preston Correspondence. South Carolina Historical Society.

Susanna Sparks Keitt Papers. South Carolina Historical Society.

Published Primary and Secondary Sources

Adams, Thomas, ed. *Germany and the Americas: Culture, Politics, and History: A Multidisciplinary Encyclopedia*. Santa Barbara, Calif.: ABC-CLIO, 2005.

Allen, Felicity. *Jefferson Davis: Unconquerable Heart*. Columbia: University of Missouri Press, 1999.

Anderson, Mary Ann, ed. *The Civil War Diary of Allen Morgan Geer, Twentieth Regiment, Illinois Volunteers*. New York: Cosmos Press, 1977.

Beckert, Sven. *The Monied Metropolis: New York City and the Consolidation of the American Bourgeoisie, 1850-1896*. New York: Cambridge University Press, 2001.

Callahan, James Morton. *The Diplomatic History of the Southern Confederacy*. Baltimore: The Johns Hopkins Press, 1901.

Case, Lynn M., and Warren F. Spencer. *The United States and France: Civil War Diplomacy*. Philadelphia: University of Pennsylvania Press, 1970.

Chesnut, Mary Boykin. *A Diary from Dixie*. Edited by Ben Ames Williams. Cambridge, Mass.: Harvard University Press, 1980.

Clay-Clopton, Virginia. *A Belle of the Fifties: Memoirs of Mrs. Clay, of Alabama*. Edited by Ada Sterling. New York: Doubleday, Page & Company, 1905.

Confederate States of America. President. *A Compilation of the Messages and Papers of the Confederacy, Including Diplomatic Correspondence, 1861-1865*. Vol. 2. Nashville, Tenn.: United States Publishing Company, 1906.

"CS Commissioner's Grave Cleaned and Marked." (June/July 2009) *Intelligence Service Europe*. http://scveuropecamp.jimdofree.com.

Culler, Daniel Marchant. *Orangeburgh District, 1768-1868: History and Records*. Spartanburg, S.C.: The Reprint Company, 1995.

Davidson, Chalmers Gaston. *The Last Foray: The South Carolina Planters of 1860: A Sociological Study*. Columbia: University of South Carolina Press, 1971.

Davis, Jefferson. *The Papers of Jefferson Davis, Volume 12, June 1865-December 1870*. Baton Rouge: Louisiana State University Press, 2008.

Davis, Jefferson. *The Papers of Jefferson Davis, Volume 13, 1871-1879*. Baton Rouge: Louisiana State University Press, 2012.

Davis, Jefferson. *The Papers of Jefferson Davis, Volume 14, 1880-1889*. Baton Rouge: Louisiana State University Press, 2015.

Davis, Varina. *Jefferson Davis, Ex-President of the Confederate States of America: A Memoir*. Baltimore, MD: The Nautical & Aviation Publishing Company of America, 1990.

Dewitt, David Miller. *The Impeachment and Trial of Andrew Johnson, Seventeenth President of the United States: A History*. New York: The Macmillan Company, 1903.

Herd, Elmer D., ed. "Sue Sparks Keitt to a Northern Friend, March 4, 1861." *South Carolina Historical Magazine,* 62 (April 1961): 82-87.

Hesseltine, William B. *A History of the South, 1607-1936,* New York: Prentice-Hall, Inc., 1941.

Johnson, Ludwell H. *North Against South: The American Iliad, 1848-1877.* Columbia, S.C.: The Foundation for American Education, 2002.

Katz, Philip M. *From Appomattox to Montmartre: Americans and the Paris Commune.* Cambridge, Mass.: Harvard University Press, 1998.

LeConte, Emma. *When the World Ended: The Diary of Emma LeConte.* Edited by Earl Schenck Miers. Lincoln: University of Nebraska Press, 1957.

Leroy, Hubert. "Ambrose Dudley Mann: Diplomat of the Lost Cause." trans. Gerald Hawkins. Confederate Historical Association of Belgium. http://chab-belgium.com/pdf/english/Mann.pdf.

Mann, Ambrose Dudley. *"My Ever Dearest Friend," The Letters of A. Dudley Mann to Jefferson Davis, 1869-1889.* Tuscaloosa, Ala.: Confederate Publishing Company, 1960.

Mann, Ambrose Dudley. "Southern Direct Trade with Europe." *DeBow's Review,* 24 (May 1858): 352-376.

Mann, George Sumner. *Mann Memorial. A Record of the Mann Family in America.* Boston: Press of D. Clapp & Son, 1884.

Marx, Karl. *The Civil War in France: Address of the General Council of the International Working-Men's Association.* London: E. Truelove, 1871.

Merchant, Holt. *South Carolina Fire-Eater: The Life of Laurence Massillon Keitt.* Columbia: University of South Carolina Press, 2014.

Miller, Thomas Condit. *West Virginia and Its People.* Vol. 3. New York: Lewis Historical Publishing Company, 1913.

Notes and Queries: A Medium of Intercommunication for Literary Men, General Readers, Etc., vol. 10, London, 1901.

Owsley, Frank Lawrence. *King Cotton Diplomacy: Foreign Relations of the Confederate States of America*. Chicago: University of Chicago Press, 1959.

Perrin, William Henry. *History of Bourbon, Scott, Harrison and Nicholas Counties, Kentucky*. Chicago: O. L. Baskin & Co., 1882.

Phelps, W. Chris. *The Bombardment of Charleston, 1863-1865*. Gretna, La.: Pelican Publishing Company, 2002.

Pryor, Sara Agnes Rice. *Reminiscences of Peace and War*. New York: The Macmillan Company, 1905.

Ross, Fitzgerald. *Cities and Camps of the Confederate States*. Chicago: University of Illinois Press, 1997.

Rutledge, David J. "Elizabeth Jamison's Tale of the War." *South Carolina Historical Magazine,* 99 (October 1998) :312-339.

Shull, Hugh. *A Guide Book of Southern States Currency*. Atlanta, Ga.: Whitman Publishing, 2007.

Sifakis, Stewart. *Who Was Who in the Civil War*. New York: Facts on File, 1988.

Stephenson, Nathaniel Wright. *An American History*. New York: Ginn and Company, 1917.

Stokes, Karen. *Confederate South Carolina: True Stories of Civilians, Soldiers and the War*. Charleston, S.C.: The History Press, 2015.

"The Life of a Diplomat." *Savannah Morning News*, August 16, 1896.

Thomas, J. A. W. *A History of Marlboro County, with Traditions and Sketches of Numerous Families*. Baltimore: Regional Publishing Company, 1978.

Thomson, David Kelley. "Bonds of War: The Evolution of World Financial Markets in the Civil War Era." PhD diss., University of Georgia, 2016.

Tyler, David Budlong. *Steam Conquers the Atlantic*. New York: D. Appleton-Century Company, 1939.

Updike, John. *Buchanan Dying: A Play*. New York: Alfred A. Knopf, 1974.

Vanauken, Sheldon. *The Glittering Illusion: English Sympathy for the Southern Confederacy*. Washington, D.C.: Regnery Gateway, 1989.

Wallace, David Duncan. *South Carolina: A Short History*. Columbia: University of South Carolina Press, 1969.

Walters, John B. *Merchant of Terror: General Sherman and Total War*. New York: Bobbs-Merrill Company, 1973.

Watterson, Henry. *"Marse Henry": An Autobiography*. New York: George H. Doran Company, 1919.

ABOUT THE EDITOR

KAREN STOKES, an archivist at the South Carolina Historical Society in Charleston, is the prolific author of over a dozen history books about South Carolina and its people during the War Between the States, all based on primary manuscript sources. These include, among others, *South Carolina Civilians in Sherman's Path, The Immortal 600, A Confederate Englishman, Confederate South Carolina, Days of Destruction, A Legion of Devils: Sherman in South Carolina*, and *Fortunes of War: The Adventures of a German Confederate*. She has also written works of historical fiction published by Shotwell including *Belles, Carolina Love Letters, The Immortals*, and *Honor in the Dust*.

Best Sellers and New Releases

Over 90 Titles For You To Enjoy

SHOTWELLPUBLISHING.COM

THE SOUTH'S FINEST CONTEMPORARY AUTHORS.

Shotwell Publishing is proud to be called home by many of today's most respected Southern scholars and literary greats.

JEFFERY ADDICOTT
Union Terror: Debunking the False Justifications for Union Terror

Trampling Union Terror: Riders of the Second Alabama Cavalry

MARK ATKINS
Women in Combat: Feminism Goes to War

JOYCE BENNETT
Maryland, My Maryland: The Cultural Cleansing of a Small Southern State

GARRY BOWERS
Slavery and The Civil War: What Your History Teacher Didn't Tell You

Dixie Days: Reminiscences Of a Southern Boyhood

JERRY BREWER
Dismantling the Republic

ANDREW P. CALHOUN
My Own Darling Wife: Letters From A Confederate Volunteer

JOHN CHODES
Segregation: Federal Policy or Racism?

Washington's KKK: The Union League During Southern Reconstruction

WALTER BRIAN CISCO
War Crimes Against Southern Civilians

DAVID T. CRUM
Stonewall Jackson: Saved by Providence

JOHN DEVANNY
Continuities: The South in a Time of Revolution

Lincoln's Continuing Revolution: Essays of M.E. Bradford and Thomas H. Landess

JOSHUA DOGGRELL
Doxed: The Political Lynching of a Southern Cop

JAMES C. EDWARDS
What Really Happened?: Quantrill's Raid On Lawrence, Kansas

TED EHMANN
Boom & Bust In Bone Valley: Florida's Phosphate Mining History 1886-2021

JOHN AVERY EMISON
The Deep State Assassination of Martin Luther King Jr.

DON GORDON
Snowball's Chance: My Kidneys Failed, My Wife Left Me & My Dog Died...

JOHN R. GRAHAM
Constitutional History of Secession

PAUL C. GRAHAM
Confederaphobia

When The Yankees Come: Former Carolina Slaves Remember

Nonsense on Stilts: The Gettysburg Address & Lincoln's Imaginary Nation

JOE D. HAINES
The Diary of Col. John Henry Stover Funk of the Stonewall Brigade, 1861-1862

CHARLES HAYES
The REAL First Thanksgiving

V.P. HUGHES
Col. John Singleton Mosby: In the News 1862-1916

TERRY HULSEY
25 Texas Heroes

*The Constitution of Non-State Government:
Field Guide to Texas Secession*

JOSEPH JAY
*Sacred Conviction:
The South's Stand for Biblical Authority*

JAMES R. KENNEDY
Dixie Rising: Rules For Rebels

*Nullifying Federal and State Gun Control:
A How-To Guide For Gun Owners*

*When Rebel Was Cool:
Growing Up In Dixie, 1950-1965*

*Reconstruction: Destroying the Republic
and Creating an Empire*

WALTER D. KENNEDY
The South's Struggle: America's Hope

*Lincoln, The Non-Christian President:
Exposing The Myth*

Lincoln, Marx, and the GOP

J.R. & W.D. KENNEDY
*Jefferson Davis: High Road to Emancipation
and Constitutional Government*

*Yankee Empire:
Aggressive Abroad and Despotic at Home*

Punished With Poverty: The Suffering South

The South Was Right! 3rd Edition

LEWIS LIBERMAN
Snowflake Buddies; ABC Leftism For Kids!

PHILIP LEIGH
*The Devil's Town: Hot Springs During
The Gangster Era*

U.S. Grant's Failed Presidency

The Causes of the Civil War

*The Dreadful Frauds: Critical Race Theory
And Identity Politics*

JACK MARQUARDT
*Around The World In 80 Years: Confessions
of a Connecticut Confederate*

MICHAEL MARTIN
Southern Grit: Sensing The Siege at Petersburg

SAMUEL MITCHAM
*The Greatest Lynching In American History:
New York, 1863*

*Confederate Patton: Richard Taylor and
The Red River Campaign*

CHARLES T. PACE
Lincoln As He Really Was

*Southern Independence. Why War? The War
To Prevent Southern Independence*

JAMES R. ROESCH
From Founding Fathers To Fire Eaters

KIRKPATRICK SALE
*Emancipation Hell: The Tragedy Wrought
By Lincoln's Emancipation Proclamation*

JOSEPH SCOTCHIE
*The Asheville Connection:
The Making of a Conservative*

ANNE W. SMITH
Charlottesville Untold: Inside Unite The Right

Robert E. Lee: A History for Kids

KAREN STOKES
A Legion Of Devils: Sherman In South Carolina

The Burning of Columbia, S.C.: A Review of Northern Assertions and Southern Facts

Carolina Love Letters

Fortunes of War: The Adventures of a German Confederate

A Confederate in Paris: Letters of A. Dudley Mann 1867-1879

JOSEPH R. STROMBERG
Southern Story and Song: Country Music in the 20th Century

JACK TROTTER
Last Train to Dixie

JOHN THEURSAM
Key West's Civil War

H.V. TRAYWICK, JR.
Along The Shadow Line: A Road Trip through History and Memory on the Old Confederate Border

LESLIE TUCKER
Old Times There Should Not Be Forgotten: Cultural Genocide In Dixie

JOHN VINSON
Southerner Take Your Stand!

MARK R. WINCHELL
Confessions of a Copperhead: Culture and Politics in the Modern South

CLYDE N. WILSON
Calhoun: A Statesman for the 21st Century

Lies My Teacher Told Me: The True History of the War For Southern Independence

The Yankee Problem: An American Dilemma

Annals Of The Stupid Party: Republicans Before Trump

Nullification: Reclaiming The Consent of the Governed

The Old South: 50 Essential Books

The War Between The States: 60 Essential Books

Reconstruction and the New South, 1865-1913: 50 Essential Books

The South 20th Century And Beyond: 50 Essential Books

Southern Poets and Poems, 1606-1860: The Land They Loved, Volume 1

Confederate Poets and Poems, Vol1 The Land They Loved, Volume II

Looking For Mr. Jefferson

African American Slavery in Historical Perspective

JOE WOLVERTON
What Degree Of Madness?: Madison's Method To Make American States Again

WALTER KIRK WOOD
Beyond Slavery: The Northern Romantic Nationalist Origins of America's Civil War

SHOTWELLPUBLISHING.COM

Green Altar (Literary Imprint)

CATHARINE SAVAGE BROSMAN
An Aesthetic Education and Other Stories (2nd Ed)

Chained Tree, Chained Owls: Poems

Aerosols and Other Poems

Partial Memoirs

RANDALL IVEY
A New England Romance: And Other Southern Stories

The Gift of Gab

SUZANNE JOHNSON
Maxcy Gregg's Sporting Journals 1842-1858

JAMES E. KIBLER, JR.
Tiller : Claybank County Series, Vol. 4

The Gentler Gamester

In the Deep Heart's Core: Poems of Tribute and Remembrance (forthcoming)

THOMAS MOORE
A Fatal Mercy: The Man Who Lost The Civil War

PERRIN LOVETT
The Substitute, Tom Ironsides 1

KAREN STOKES
Belles

Carolina Twilight

Honor in the Dust

The Immortals

The Soldier's Ghost: A Tale of Charleston

WILLIAM THOMAS
Runaway Haley: An Imagined Family Saga

The Field of Justice: Moonshine and Murder in North Georgia

CLYDE N. WILSON
Southern Poets and Poems, 1606-1860: The Land They Loved, Volume 1

Confederate Poets and Poems, Vol1 The Land They Loved, Volume II

Gold-Bug
(Mystery & Suspense Imprint)

BRANDI PERRY
Splintered: A New Orleans Tale

MARTIN WILSON
To Jekyll and Hide

Free Book Offer

Don't get left out, y'all.

Sign-up and be the first to know about new releases, sales, and other goodies —plus we'll send you TWO FREE EBOOKS!

Lies My Teacher Told Me:
The True History of the War for
Southern Independence
by Dr. Clyde N. Wilson

When The Yankees Come
Former Carolina Slaves Remember
Sherman's March From the Sea
by Paul C. Graham

FreeLiesBook.com

Southern Books. No Apologies.
We love the South — its history, traditions, and culture — and are proud of our inheritance as Southerners. Our books are a reflection of this love.

www.ingramcontent.com/pod-product-compliance
Lightning Source LLC
Chambersburg PA
CBHW051128160426
43195CB00014B/2388